The
Canterbury Tales
A Literary Pilgrimage

The

Canterbury Tales

A Literary Pilgrimage

David Williams

Twayne Publishers • Boston
A Division of G. K. Hall & Co.

THE CANTERBURY TALES:
A LITERARY PILGRIMAGE

David Williams

Twayne's Masterwork Studies
No. 4

Copyright © 1987 by G. K. Hall & Co.
All Rights Reserved
Published by Twayne Publishers
A Division of G. K. Hall & Co.
70 Lincoln Street, Boston, Massachusetts 02111

Designed and produced by Marne B. Sultz
Copyediting supervised by Lewis DeSimone
Typeset in Sabon with Plantin Light display type
by Compset, Inc., Beverly, Massachusetts

Printed on permanent/durable acid-free paper
and bound in the United States of America

First Printing

Library of Congress Cataloging in Publication Data

Williams, David (David Eliot), 1939–
The Canterbury Tales.

(Twayne's masterwork studies ; no. 4)
Bibliography: p. 109
Includes index.
1. Chaucer, Geoffrey, d. 1400. Canterbury tales.
2. Chaucer, Geoffrey, d. 1400—Philosophy.
3. Nominalism in literature. I. Title. II. Series.
PR1874.W55 1987   821'.1   86-29486
ISBN 0-8057-7952-3
ISBN 0-8057-8004-1 (pbk.)

Contents

Note on References and Acknowledgments

All citations of the *Canterbury Tales* are from F. N. Robinson, ed., *The Works of Geoffrey Chaucer,* 2d ed. (Boston: Houghton Mifflin, 1957). Modern English equivalents to Middle English are given in parentheses where it was thought helpful.

I would like to acknowledge first and foremost the work of my research assistant, Mr. Robert Myles, who participated in all aspects of the preparation of this book with diligence, intelligence, and critical acumen. I would also like to thank Professor Douglas Wurtele of Carleton University, who read the manuscript and provided helpful comments, and Miss Anna Williams, who prepared the diagram in chapter 3. I am grateful to Ms. Valentina Matsangos for proofreading the text, Mr. Brian Morel for technical assistance, and Mr. Kendall Wallis, Reference Department, McLennan Library, McGill University, for his valuable assistance. I would like to acknowledge as well the generous support of the Graduate Faculty, McGill University.

The Ellesmere portrait of Chaucer. Huntington MS 26.C.9.
Huntington Library, San Marino, California.

Chronology: Geoffrey Chaucer's Life and Works

1327	Edward III accedes to the throne.
ca. 1340–1345	Geoffrey Chaucer born, in London, to John Chaucer, a prosperous wine merchant, and Agnes de Copton.
1348	In June, a rat on board ship from France carries a flea bearing the bacterium of the Black Plague into the port of Malcom Regis, Dorset. In the next eighteen months, 25 to 50 percent of the population dies of bubonic and pneumonic plague. Shortage of manpower contributes to the collapse of the feudal system in England.
ca. 1355	Serves as page to countess of Ulster, wife of duke of Clarence, second son of Edward III.
1360	Captured while on military service in France; ransomed by Edward III.
1366	Marries Phillipa Roet, sister of Katherine Swynford, mistress and, later, third wife of John of Gaunt.
1367	Becomes yeoman in the king's household.
1369	Promoted to esquire in the king's household. *The Book of the Duchess* probably written for Blanche, the first wife of John of Gaunt, who died in this year.
1370–1378	Travels extensively on the Continent on the king's business. Has the occasion to meet many of the leading European literary figures of the day, including Boccaccio.
1374–1385	Controller of Customs for the Port of London, an important and responsible position. Customs duties were the main source of revenue for the king; because these had to be approved by Parliament, the power of Parliament increased.
1377	Richard II accedes to the throne.
1378–1417	Great Schism of the Papacy.
ca. 1379–1380	Writes *The House of Fame*.
1381	The Peasant's Revolt.

ca. 1381–1383	Writes *The Parliament of Fowls*.
1382–1385	Translates Boethius's *Consolation of Philosophy*. Writes *Troilus and Criseyde*.
1385	Appointed Justice of the Peace for Kent.
1386	Elected to Parliament.
1387	Wife dies.
ca. 1387–1400	Writes the *Canterbury Tales*.
1389–1400	Receives various appointments and grants.
1399	Richard II deposed and murdered; Henry IV crowned. Ceremony conducted in English for the first time since the Norman Conquest.
1400	Chaucer dies 25, October; buried in Westminster Cathedral. Around his tomb, "Poet's Corner" grows through the centuries.

· 1 ·

Historical Context

Geoffrey Chaucer was no ordinary man.[1] Chaucer's literary career was only one aspect of his life. He held various positions in a royal household from an early age; he was captured while on military service in France and was ransomed by the king; his marriage may have been strategic—his wife's sister was the mistress and later the wife of the powerful John of Gaunt, an influential ally; for many years he traveled all over the Continent on diplomatic missions for the king; he held important government positions, such as the Collector of Customs for the City of London; he was elected to Parliament; he was touched by sexual scandal (he may have been guilty of rape or, perhaps, was merely being pursued for child support by a paramour); he lived through the Black Death and its many subsequent epidemics.

Geoffrey Chaucer's outwardly active public life was matched by a lively and profound inward life. His literary works show that he was extremely well-read; the works of Virgil, Cicero, Ovid, Boethius, Dante, and Boccaccio were among his favorites, many of them in their original languages. Indeed, he translated major texts of philosophy and literature from Latin and French into English. His treatise on the astrolabe shows his interests in practical science, and his works are strewn with metaphors and allusions drawn from medicine, law, astrology, music, and biblical exegesis.

From all this we might conclude that Chaucer spread himself rather thin—that he was a dilettante—but the opposite is true. The major thinkers and creators of the Middle Ages did not specialize as we do today. While we think of Chaucer as a poet before all else, in the Middle Ages poetry and the other arts were part of a larger whole of "sciences," which together guided the human mind as far as it could go toward a true perception of the nature of reality. And it is this, *the nature of reality,* which was a fundamental subject of concern of

Chaucer's poetry. Philosophy was the foundation of his art.[2] Chaucer was well aware of the conflicting views of reality current in his day, which, with some transformations and renaming, are still current in our own day.

All the "Chaucers" mentioned above—the courtier, the soldier, the diplomat, the man of great learning, the man-of-the-world who survived and succeeded through his acute understanding of human nature and personality—are the authors of his works. But when we examine his greatest canvas, the *Canterbury Tales,* the Geoffrey Chaucer who encompasses all these Chaucers is the man concerned with the nature of reality and the function of man and his work within that reality, or those realities.

The Fourteenth Century

In the history of English literature there have been moments of transition—of rapid change, and transformation in the manner and subject matter of the aesthetic apprehension of reality. The first three decades of our own century represented such a moment, as did the period of the great Romantic poets, and the reign of Elizabeth I. Such a moment, too, was the period in England neatly bracketed by the dates of Geoffrey Chaucer—ca. 1340–1400.

Chaucer lived in a cultural golden age within the vast period we call the Middle Ages. Heirs to the artistic and intellectual monuments left by Augustine, Boethius, Aquinas, Virgil, Ovid, Dante, and many more, the writers of the fourteenth century were well placed to attempt a final, eloquent expression of the medieval worldview, which as a synthesis of the Classical and Christian-Hebrew philosophical traditions, constitutes one of the great achievements of the human mind and spirit.[3]

During this period we witness not just a rebirth and transformation of the vital artistic impulses, not just a renaissance or a revolution in English letters, but also the spectacularly sudden, first complete flowering of a magnificent national, vernacular literature. Literature was to be the art form in which the English would distinguish themselves above all others, and it all really begins in the period that must be called the age of Geoffrey Chaucer. His literary star dominates the constellation of European literature of the period; he is rivaled only by Dante, who wrote earlier in the century.

In the English sky, lesser but nonetheless brilliant lights also distinguished themselves. Perhaps the finest single poem of the period is *Pearl*. Its anonymous author, known aptly as "the *Pearl* poet," also wrote one of the finest romances of English and European literature— *Sir Gawain and the Green Knight*. Working directly with the theme of salvation and its obstacles, William Langland in *Piers Plowman* gives us a very complete and often cutting series of portraits of the people and the temper of the period. There was also a large body of homiletic literature—prose sermons for preachers. While most of these are not of great literary interest, they sparked an interest in translating the Bible, the final product of which was the high-quality, Wycliffe-inspired, complete translation upon which the later authorized version was to be based. The mystical revival of the period produced one good writer of English prose, Walter Hilton, and one great writer, the anonymous author of *The Cloud of Unknowing*.

Why do we witness such a sudden and dramatic effusion of fine literary productions in the English language? We might apply what Herbert Read calls his "axiom in art history"; that is, "*always expect a constant aesthetic factor,*" and if there is a change, "*look for the external forces that transform it.*"[4] The external forces that are reflected in, or that cause, change, transformation, and development in the artistic representation of this period are many. For the fourteenth century in Europe generally, the Black Death and the problems of the papacy—the so-called Babylonian Captivity (1309–77) and the Great Schism (1378–1415)—immediately come to mind. For England, in particular, of great consequence was the Hundred Years' War (1337–1453) with France, which permanently affected all aspects of English life. These events deserve much more detailed description than can be offered here, and the reader would be well advised to consult the literature on these subjects.[5]

By the end of Chaucer's period in England we see a new pride in nation and in English as national language. With this pride came a higher status for literature written in English. This new status is well symbolized by the fact that in 1399, when Henry IV laid claim to the throne, he did so not in French, as had his predecessors, but in English, the language that his friend Geoffrey Chaucer had done so much to establish as a medium capable of the highest artistic expression and, hence, worthy to be used on the most significant and solemn of public occasions. While the literary production of the period may be seen as a consequence of external forces, the literary production of Geoffrey Chaucer, and particularly the *Canterbury Tales,* may be considered an event in itself, the consequences of which are still felt today.

The Intellectual Milieu

It is difficult and possibly misleading to summarize briefly a cultural period as long and as complex as the Middle Ages, but it is nevertheless true that the single term that best characterizes and embraces this era is *Christianity.* For the present purposes it is not so much the pious or devotional aspects of the Christian tradition that concern us as the intellectual, philosophical, and ethical concerns to which Christianity gave importance, and the methods it developed to deal with them. In the most general terms medieval Christianity, like other traditions, sought to describe the structure of human knowledge as well as the nature of the objects of that knowledge. Particularly important for the philosophical poet was the question of the nature of language itself, which was recognized by all medieval thinkers as a primary and privileged tool that permitted knowledge of the essential nature of reality.

The broad history of medieval intellectual thought must be traced back along roads and connecting paths that lead through space and time to ancient Palestine and Greece; from one emerges the Holy Scriptures, and from the other the monumental, all-affecting thought of Plato and Aristotle; from which we proceed to Plotinus, Augustine, and Boethius (whose principal work, *The Consolation of Philosophy,* so impressed Chaucer that he translated it from Latin into English), and into the Middle Ages, where the figures of Abelard, Aquinas, Ockham, and Dante serve as the principal signposts.

The complex history of medieval thought has been said to consist of two divergent strands, the Platonic tradition and realism on the one hand, and Aristotelianism and nominalism on the other. This is without doubt an oversimplification quite capable of misleading. It is usually forgotten that Neoplatonism, a pervasive conceptual force, is itself a confluence of Platonic and Aristotelian thought. More often than not the strands of Platonism and Aristotelianism intertwine in the same thinker. This is certainly true, for example, for both Thomas Aquinas and Dante. However, one strand or the other usually dominates. When Thomas Aquinas, the student of Aristotelian logic, turns his hand to poetic expression, his hymns, like his great philosophical and theological writings, are notable for their conceptual clarity rather than for their metaphoric or decorative language. In contrast, the verse of Dante, in its rich and complex language, images, and description manifests a deep Christian Neoplatonic influence.

To the medieval thinker (and Chaucer, of course, was one of them) human experience is an intellectual and moral journey toward the source of being called God. All medieval Christian thinkers agree that the human mind cannot ever fully know God, but that through the refinement of the mind, and the body as well, significant progress along the road of knowing can be made. There are disagreements about how far along that road one can go and, especially, about the best means to go by. During the fourteenth century, the position developed that language in its rhetorical and metaphoric mode is not only a more limited means of understanding than other, more empirical, ways, but also that it hinders us in truly understanding even those phenomena of the world which are well within the scope of human cognition. Especially in its extreme, postmedieval forms, such a view does not place much value on poetry, or on art generally.

While insisting on the ultimate need to rise above language and all other discourses, "to know" in the fullest sense, another tradition of the Middle Ages values language precisely in its symbolic dimension as the most effective means to this point of transcendence. It is not surprising that many of the Christian thinkers who choose poetry as a means of exploring and possessing reality find themselves in this latter tradition, but it would hardly be true to say that they all do. A source of fascination in Chaucer's work is, as has been said, the fact that perhaps he alone in the Middle Ages makes the problem of the function of language and poetry the very subject of his poetry. In the *Canterbury Tales* Chaucer takes delight in persistently calling attention to the art of manipulating language within poetic structure, and skillfully demonstrates alternative modes of poetic form.

The great artistic achievement of the Middle Ages, and perhaps especially of the fourteenth century, is the development of allegory, both in literary works and in other aesthetic forms. Allegory is an important subject in the study of Chaucer. Because he used the form in such a subtle way one must be careful to discern when he intends allegorical meanings and when he does not.

In the fourteenth century, textual allegory ranges from works that develop what are to us tedious and facile correspondences to others that to this day are numbered among our greatest pieces of literature. If we compare Prudentius's *Psychomachia*, in which simple abstractions are personified and dramatized, to Dante's *Divine Comedy*, in which figures embody increasingly rich sets of relations and centers of meaning, something of the range and richness of allegorical poetry may be seen, and few of us will hesitate in preferring Dante. In a letter to his patron Can Grande della Scala, for whom he was trying to explain the workings of his *Divine Comedy*, Dante provides an explanation of the way in which he sees allegory and how he himself has developed the allegorical mode: "For the elucidation, therefore, of what we have to say, it must be understood that the meaning of this work is not of one kind only; rather the work may be described as 'polysemous,' that is, having several meanings."[6]

The polysemous nature of allegory is one in which not only different levels of meaning may be found but, in addition, seemingly limitless relations of sets of meanings to other sets of meanings may be discovered, all leading back, or "up," to a center of meaning that is renewed each time it is reencountered.

Chaucer benefited greatly from what appears to be a profound understanding of what Dante was doing in the *Divine Comedy,* and the debt should be clearly recognized. Chaucer, however, is no mere imitator. In the English poet's hands, polysemous allegory develops in directions not explored by its Italian originator.

· 2 ·

The *Canterbury Tales* and the Tradition of English Literature

The Importance of the Work

A question often asked about the literature of the Middle Ages, as well as the literature before and just after it, is why we read it at all. Chaucer wrote the *Canterbury Tales* six hundred years ago in a form of English that is, when we encounter it for the first time, difficult to understand (although most readers adapt to Middle English with surprising speed). Chaucer also described a world that was, at least on the surface, vastly different from ours. Why should we go to the trouble of reading a text such as the *Canterbury Tales?*

The answers to this question are many, but particularly with the *Canterbury Tales*, they can all be distilled to one word: pleasure. It would be difficult to name any other single work that offers the range of pleasures that one may experience while reading the *Canterbury Tales*. From the aesthetic pleasure of reading (preferably aloud) some of the finest poetry ever written in any language, to the belly laugh of slapstick comedy, the *Canterbury Tales* is a cornucopia of delights. One may also find pleasure in satisfying a historical curiosity we all have about our biography, and if English is our mother tongue, no matter what our ethnic or racial origin may be, the biography of the English language and people are part of our own biographies.

Linked with this idea of our personal biographies is one of the greatest pleasures we encounter in reading the *Canterbury Tales*: discovering how people felt and thought about various moral, intellectual, and philosophical topics (they are all interrelated). This can be, at once, a fascinating, instructive, and surprising exercise, because we discover so much about ourselves and our society and how we have come to think the way we think. Our ways of viewing reality develop out of a long continuum of people and culture, and we are often surprised in reading the *Canterbury Tales* to discover how few of our concerns are fundamentally new and how few of our solutions are original.

In the *Canterbury Tales* Chaucer shows us the moral struggle of men and women. The characters he created are historically centuries removed, but, through great art, are present here and now. Some of these characters were struggling to balance their personal responsibility with the need for individual liberty; others, their self-interest with their concern for others. Some were responding to the demands of reason and of passion; still others were questioning these demands. Some were looking to nature and science for a guide to life; others were vegetating and marking time. Looking back through six centuries and seeing ourselves can be a dizzying, exhilarating, and humbling experience.

We are also humbled by finding ourselves in the presence of an artistic genius of great skill and vast knowledge. While admiring the artist's skills in poetics and rhetoric, and while quite happy to enjoy his great comic ability, we still ask to what end Chaucer used them. That he wished to entertain, to give pleasure, is indisputable, but how refined is the entertainment? The detailed answer to this question will demonstrate that Chaucer is a philosophical poet unrivaled in his ability to blend intellectual perception with imaginative creation.

The *Canterbury Tales* has had an enormous influence on successive writers and audiences[7] because it transmits one of the most brilliant illuminations of human experience—social, intellectual, and spiritual—that we possess. The poem has also maintained an important place in the tradition because in its illumination of the human experience it reflects upon the function of art and language in that experience—a pervasive concern of thinkers and artists for all times.

Critical Reception

Unlike some poetic geniuses, Chaucer was a literary hero in his own day and, while still living, was paid the supreme compliment of being imitated. Moreover, while many great literary figures have had their reputations wax and wane as periods of literary taste change, Chaucer's high reputation has largely remained constant through the centuries.

The very first recorded tribute to Chaucer is by his French contemporary Eustache Deschamps, who, about 1368, pays the English poet an elegant compliment in which he describes Chaucer as a Socrates in philosophy, a Seneca in morals, and an Ovid in poetry. Such descriptions not only help us understand the kind of reputation Chaucer had in his own day but also suggest that by the fourteenth century there existed an international school of poetry very conscious of the importance of art and ready to make bold claims for its theoretical foundation.

In his own time Chaucer's work was already a model for other artists, and Chaucerian "schools" grew up soon after his death. The *Canterbury Tales* in particular was imitated, and several poets of the fifteenth century expanded the original work by adding to it tales of their own creation. The so-called Scottish Chaucerians included King James I of Scotland, who, while imprisoned in England, wrote verse influenced by Chaucer.

An important fact not always given sufficient emphasis in discussion of Chaucer is that he is the first native English literary authority, and the extent of his authority is unequaled in English literature. This is due, in part, to Chaucer's own awareness of the importance of his canon, his entire literary production, in forming a beginning to a larger, ever-growing English literary canon. Again and again Chaucer reflects upon the state of his art and authorship; this conscious tradition making seems to have found a response in later poets.

Chaucer is repeatedly referred to in the fifteenth and sixteenth centuries as "Master" by aspiring and established writers alike. In his *Apology for Poetry* (1595), Sir Philip Sidney firmly established Chaucer (along with Gower) as the wellspring of English poetry: "I know not whether to marvel more, either that he in that misty time could see so clearly, or that we in this clear age walk so stumblingly after him." Edmund Spenser, in *The Shepheardes Calendar* (1579), finds advantage in describing himself as the literary descendant of Chaucer. Shakespeare, who never mentions Chaucer, was clearly influenced by his predecessor's work, especially by *Troilus and Criseyde* and the *Canterbury Tales.*

Dryden and Pope in the late seventeenth and early eighteenth centuries were quite explicit in their admiration of the master and devoted themselves to modernizing his work and publishing their versions of many of the tales. During the Enlightenment, Chaucer offered, in addition to his artistry, an English poet sufficiently antique to be regarded as a native authority within an ideology based on the authority of the past. This is perhaps most clear in Dryden's "Preface" to *Fables, Ancient and Modern,* in which he groups Chaucer's *Canterbury Tales* with the works of Ovid, while preferring "the Englishman to the Roman."

In the nineteenth century, interestingly enough, it is for different reasons that Chaucer maintains his position of prestige within the tradition. Chaucer's naturalness and freedom from contrivance is what many of the Romantic poets admire in his work. Keats, for example, imitates the poetry and language of the *Canterbury Tales* to evoke a "medieval" tone in "The Eve of Saint Mark." William Blake, in his illustration of the *Canterbury Tales,* provides a kind of visual interpretation of the poem that is typically nineteenth century. Coleridge not only extravagantly praises Chaucer but also explicitly prefers Chaucer to Shakespeare, for reasons of Romantic ideology. "The sympathy of the poet with the subjects of his poetry is particularly remarkable in Shakespeare and Chaucer; but what the first effects by a strong act of the imagination and mental metamorphosis, the last does without any effort, merely by the inborn kindly joyousness of his nature. How well we seem to know Chaucer! How absolutely nothing do we know of Shakespeare!"

In the modern period, Ezra Pound was another poet who preferred Chaucer to Shakespeare (he also preferred Chaucer to Dante), because "Chaucer had a deeper knowledge of life than Shakespeare."[8] It is interesting to note how often the question of relative superiority arises in poets' discussions of these two literary ancestors. The somewhat

"As Newton numbered the stars, and as Linneus numbered the plants, so Chaucer numbered the classes of men." William Blake, The Canterbury Pilgrims, *1809. Lawrence Lande Blake Collection. McGill University Library. Rare Books Department.*

provocative statements of preference for Chaucer over Shakespeare seem to have to do with a desire to challenge and rearrange the canon of English literary tradition while at the same time reinforcing its existence.

Probably the best-known use of the *Canterbury Tales* by a modern author is found in the opening lines of T. S. Eliot's *The Waste Land*, which begins:

> April is the cruellest month, breeding
> Lilacs out of the dead land, mixing
> Memory and desire, stirring
> Dull roots with spring rain.
> (1–4)[9]

and continues to paraphrase the opening lines of Chaucer's *General Prologue*, while inverting their sense. Eliot seems to have here understood and wished to continue in his own work the medieval practice of *translatio*, in which the artist revives literary monuments of the past by integrating or "translating" them into his own work and culture, giving them new or transformed meanings.

Modern scholarly criticism of the *Canterbury Tales* may be said to begin with George Lyman Kittredge,[10] who established in the first decade of the twentieth century an interpretive view of Chaucer's work which, in its general outlines, dominated at least the next forty years of Chaucer scholarship. While the Kittredgian view today seems rather outmoded and old-fashioned in its critical assumptions, it had the virtue of treating Chaucer's poetry as literature rather than as philology, that is, as historically interesting written records. Briefly, Kittredge perceived two features of the *Canterbury Tales*. He pointed to the use of certain general themes in the tales around which individual tales were clustered, creating among the pilgrims a form of debate on the given theme. Thus, Kittredge explained, we see certain tales whose subject, generally, is marriage, its woes and joys; they are the *Wife of Bath's Tale*, the *Clerk's Tale*, the *Merchant's Tale*, and the *Franklin's Tale*. These form for Kittredge the famous "marriage group." Equally influential for later critics was Kittredge's view that the *Canterbury Tales* was an essentially dramatic poem depending, like all conventional drama, on the similarity of the dramatic action of the poem to human life and real human situations. Thus, for Kittredge, Chaucer's triumph was to be found in his realism, and for his successors the "portraits" of the *Canterbury Tales* achieve greatness by creating characters who are memorable, psychologically accurate, true to life, or even larger than life. In this school of criticism art imitates life in a simple manner, and Chaucer's art becomes, for the least imaginative of these critics, accurate reportage of actual events, personally observed. That these portraits seemed to resemble characters based on the cultural assumptions of the twentieth century, far more than those of Chaucer's own times, eventually raised the suspicion and doubt of later critics. But Kittredge's great scholarship and sensibilities allowed him to change the course of Chaucer study. Along with C. S. Lewis, who, in the modern period, reintroduced students to the essential question of medieval allegory, Kittredge reclaimed Chaucer from the philologists as a subject for serious literary consideration.

Although several scholars in the forties and fifties contributed important corrective studies that transcended the limitations of Kittredge's realism,[11] the next scholar to define and transform in a fundamental and thorough way, not only Chaucer scholarship but medieval literary study, is D. W. Robertson. With the publication of *A Preface to Chaucer* in 1962,[12] Robertson created a turmoil in medieval studies that has lasted more than twenty years. It is a measure of his contribution that he transformed our ways of talking about Chaucer and his age either by exciting enthusiastic devotion to his views or ferocious resistance. Robertson's theory as applied to Chaucer and several other medieval subjects is based on historical criticism and insists on the necessity of placing Chaucer in the context of his own cultural and intellectual milieu. Thus the Robertsonians brought us back to nonliterary, primarily philosophical and theological texts, in order to understand the structure, imagery, and intellectual content of medieval poetry. Robertson's own massive scholarship described medieval aesthetics as one in which the central intellectual and moral concept was the Christian theory of charity, and he identified that idea as the central theme of Chaucer's work and all other serious medieval poetry.

Robertson's critical stance was in its time an important and necessary antidote to what seemed an increasingly impressionistic style of criticism. It was also a somewhat severe form of historicism which insisted that medieval aesthetics, and only medieval aesthetics, was the legitimate critical tool for the study of medieval literature. Perhaps unwittingly, this opening up of the literature of the Middle Ages to other medieval intellectual fields sometimes had the effect of isolating it once again from important new developments in modern literary theory. This is somewhat ironic since in bringing us back and insisting we understand medieval aesthetic theory, it is primarily D. W. Robertson who has helped reveal the particular pertinence of medieval aesthetics to modern critical theory.

The modern critic, with the advantage of possessing the great philological and historical work done by his or her predecessors, is turning more often to contemporary literary theory in an effort to illuminate Chaucer's texts and to discover further veins of richness in the *Canterbury Tales*.

· 3 ·

The Philosophical Debate

Chaucer's philosophy was that of his time, and the word *critical* has been aptly used to characterize the philosophy of the period. "Scholastic philosophy found its mature expression during the thirteenth and fourteenth centuries. The scholasticism of the thirteenth century was predominantly receptive. . . . Their work can perhaps best be called 'synthetic'. By contrast, fourteenth-century scholasticism was occupied in sifting, revising and adapting its rich legacy of ideas. . . . Their philosophy may therefore be characterised by the term 'critical'."[13] Chaucer's approach to the philosophical problems of the period can also be called critical: he sifts and sorts, playing one side of the argument off against the other. In fact, this critical stance goes a long way toward explaining the upsurge of Chaucer's popularity in another critical age—our own. All the philosophical problems of Chaucer's time can be reduced to the critical debate between nominalism and realism, both of which can be subsumed under the "problem of the universals."[14] The debate over this problem underlies those tales which we shall examine in detail.

The problem of the universals relates to the fact that when we think, we unite many things into one concept. When we see many men or horses we form the concept "man" or "horse"; when we see many tables we form the concept "table." Concepts allow us to identify individual existing things, or aspects of these things, (for example, their color) when we meet them. I may encounter a particular horse, or man, or table that I have never seen before, but if I know the universal concept I will know that this being or thing is a table or a horse or a man. That this occurs when we think is obviously true, but why and how it occurs has been a matter of ongoing debate in Western civilization since the time of the ancient Greeks. Indeed, this problem of the universals is a subject that, consciously or unconsciously, still involves us all today. This problem is not just of academic interest, for our conscious or unconscious attitude toward universals, particulars, and their relationship defines the view we will hold of reality, the world, ourselves, and the nature of right and wrong, as well as our understanding of the nature and function of art.

In a formal debate there is a single issue, capital punishment or nuclear disarmament, for example, and two teams argue opposing views. One could word the problem to be resolved on the issue of universals in the following way: given that we form universal concepts such as man, horse, justice, and yellow, are these concepts in some way real or are they only useful names that permit us to speak of similar, but wholly individual, existing realities? In the Middle Ages those who held that universal concepts were real were called "realists," a usage quite different than what we mean by a "realist" today. Those who held that concepts were only useful names that permit us to talk about and relate various things were called nominalists, from the Latin *nomen*, "a name." Most people fell between these two camps. Those in the middle were often called "moderate realists." So that we may recognize their schools when we encounter them in the *Canterbury Tales*, let us look at a few of the major realists, moderate realists, and nominalists.

Plato is considered the first realist. Plato posited that the reason we can perceive common factors among groups of things, such as all mankind, all things that are yellow, or all just acts is that the *particulars*, such as a particular man, the yellow in a particular leaf, or a particular just act that we experience, have behind them a common *universal* idea of man, "yellow," or "justice," in which they participate. In other words, *humanness, yellowness,* and *justice* really exist somewhere and make possible men and women, yellow leaves, and just behavior.

Aristotle disagreed with Plato, but he did not go to the extreme position that denied totally that universal concepts did in some way exist. For this reason he is called a moderate realist. He is not a realist because he did not think that there was a realm where universals existed, where one found the idea of the perfect man or horse. Aristotle is not a nominalist because he said that universals existed, but that they somehow existed only in individual or particular things. The idea of man existed in this man and that man and all men taken together. While this view is easier to accept because it can be understood from our awareness that there are many men and they are all very similar, it contained its own source of confusion: how could a single universal, say the idea of table or "tablehood," be at once present in a large number of individual tables?

A realist who set the philosophical groundwork for the discussion of universals a thousand years before the age of Chaucer was Saint Augustine. As a Christian, he transformed what he retained of Plato's thought as it had been interpreted and developed by the "Platonists" of his day, the Neoplatonists. Universals became for him and his many followers realities present in the world, but realities that originated and existed most perfectly as thoughts in the mind of God. Words such as *man, yellow,* and *justice* signified real universal ideas that existed in the mind of God. This leads to the Augustinian view of language,[15] prevalent throughout the Middle Ages but challenged in Chaucer's time, which perceived an inherent signifying power in language in relation to reality. Words are signs that rightly used truly signify independently existing realities.

Thomas Aquinas, who was very much influenced by both Aristotle and Neoplatonism, was another moderate realist. God is transcendent, above this realm of existence. While God creates all things and sustains them in existence, he is so far beyond us that we can never know or say what he is. We know that God exists, says Aquinas, only from his effects: existing creatures such as ourselves. Aquinas says that universals may somehow exist in God, but that the things we see and the things we see in them, for example, Socrates and his wisdom, are not identical with some idea in the mind of God. Aquinas, like Aristotle, believes universals exist only in union with that which exists. In other words, he rejects Plato's idea of Forms.

The most important figure in medieval nominalism is William of Ockham (ca. 1290–1349). For Ockham, universals are names referring to groups of similar individual realities. These names are formed in our minds and exist only in our minds. The things named as man, or horse, or table are singular individual existing things. A name is a convenient sign that we use to connote resemblances. In its extreme form (to which Ockham did not take it) nominalism denies any objective reality at all except individual experience. There is nothing common to any group of things—men, for instance—except the word used to describe them, and no convincing reason can be given as to why other things might not also be included under the same name. Language becomes simultaneously the only truth and the most slippery, at once exalted and debased. In the hands of the ill-intentioned, the nominalist view allows truth and reality to be anything one wishes. On the other hand, nominalism leads directly to empiricism and the empirical sciences. With the emphasis on the particular phenomenon as the abode of the real, the experimental investigation of particulars was given special importance. Thus, observable fact and individual experience are the sole bases of knowledge. Nominalism in this general sense leads directly to modern science.

Even in the Middle Ages, however, the nominalist emphasis on the empirical led more often than not to skepticism. Since the similarities that exist between things, which is what allows us to have abstract concepts, are finally "only words," with no natural or absolute relation to what they signify, the progressive uncertainty about the validity of human knowledge is guaranteed. Once the arbitrariness of words is extended to reality itself, the world becomes a huge language construct. This is the topsy-turvy world of Lewis Carroll's Humpty Dumpty, an extreme nominalist, who tells Alice, "When I use a word . . . it means just what I choose it to mean." Alice takes a realist position in the medieval sense when she responds, "The question is . . . whether you *can* make words mean so many different things."[16]

The debate of Alice and Humpty Dumpty has been ongoing in Western civilization for several thousand years. Chaucer, keenly aware that the stuff of his art is words, insistently debates their relation to reality, particularly in the *Canterbury Tales*. What is the power of language? Is there a reality governing human discourse which that discourse reveals, or do words create the reality they describe? The answers to these questions determine fundamentally the way a poet approaches art, as well as the moral responsibility for its practice.

We have then the Augustinian view of language: language reveals reality; it does not create it. In this view, how we use language is extremely important; there is a true and a false way of speaking and writing. For the budding nominalist, on the other hand, language is heuristic; that is, it serves as a means to an end, as a pragmatic tool of investigation; *true* and *false*, therefore, take on a relative, rather than an absolute, meaning.

Poetry, or any fiction, is, of course, false, but for those who share the Augustinian view, its metaphoric capacity may be a means of conveying truth, when its fictiveness is made sufficiently clear so that the mind is encouraged to search out its allegorical representations. Fiction, or poetry, then, creates analogies in a symbolic world with truths and true concepts in the real world. This involves much more than simply correctly naming the thing indicated; rather, as Paul Christianson states it, "a much truer task for language is not the attempt to reduplicate the things of the world 'wher that they stonde,' but the more traditional Christian effort rather to say true things about them."[17] It is only when the literary symbol leads to a knowledge of something beyond itself that fiction can be worthwhile.

When, however, the discourse within fiction has no reference outside itself, it is nothing or lies, as Plato said and the majority of medieval thinkers repeated. But for those who adopt the view that there are no universal truths constituting reality, that everything is a linguistic fiction, then the illusion of the literary creation has equal status with the illusion of life. The literary artifact refers only to itself in the same way that nonliterary discourse reveals nothing more than its own process. While the rigorous, philosophical nominalist, interested primarily in logic, had even less use for art than its previous detractors, nominalism is also to be found in certain kinds of pro-literary attitudes. Indeed, in such views, carried to their extremes, literature is better than life since the text is completely within our control, allow-

ing full play to the generation of endless meanings without consequence or contradiction.

Today it is noteworthy that so many of the most eminent contemporary thinkers, trained originally in philosophy, psychiatry, linguis-
tics, and other disciplines, have sought out literary fiction to apply and
to demonstrate what are fundamentally nominalist theories. The Middle Ages was not innocent of this view, and in the *Canterbury Tales*
Chaucer introduces us to a number of figures who construct their tales
on such a basis. Although none of them is presented with great sympathy, their point of view is given serious consideration. Chaucer
seems to have been profoundly concerned with this general question
of the relation of poetic fiction to reality, and much of his greatness is
contained in his ability to have made of this timeless concern the very
subject of his poetry. Different versions of the relativist's position shall
be seen in our readings of the *Miller's Tale*, the *Wife of Bath's Tale*,
and the *Pardoner's Tale*. Each tale, with its prologue, represents great
artistic achievement, and, therefore, there is an inescapable irony in
Chaucer's ultimate rejection of the hypothesis that they are built upon.
In the *Nun's Priest's Tale*, it is suggested, Chaucer begins to reveal
more openly his own theory of fiction and its relation to the real.
Finally, however, Chaucer and his audiences seem to be left with the
intriguing paradox that, more often than not, bad philosophy makes
good art, a problem that Chaucer is one of the first to raise but one
he leaves open for his artistic successors.

· 4 ·

Finding the Audience

One of the most permeating ideas in medieval thought, distilled from centuries of refinement of Neoplatonic doctrine, is that things are not what they seem to be. Alanus de Insulis (ca. 1114–1202) expressed it more formally: "Every creature in the world is, for us, a book, a picture, and a mirror as well."[18] The world, and life itself, are more than the appearance of the phenomena and experiences in them, for upon sensitive scrutiny they open out into larger and larger meanings and into more and more complex relations with other phenomena. Indeed, relations, connections, analogies between things and ideas provide the key to the transcendence of appearance toward reality. While, for the medieval thinker, things are not what they seem to be, neither are they just anything that the observer may want them to be, nor, finally, are they meaningless. Rather, the world is so meaningful that it demands a recognition of its own rich complexity through an elaborate process of intellectual and emotional pilgrimage. At the end of that process, however, resides a reality that is absolutely simple, so simple in fact that it is finally inexpressible because language itself, even at its most basic, is still too complex. This is, of course, a paradox, and the paradoxical element of medieval thought is pervasive. While the modern concepts of "point of view" and "ambiguity" are similar to medieval rhetorical concepts, they are still different in the assumptions that lie behind them, for while, in general, the modern use of ambiguity arises out of a concession that there is nothing to know, the medieval employment of paradox reflects a conviction as to the absolute meaningfulness and realness of everything that is known and unknown.

Perhaps no medieval poet as much as Chaucer demonstrates this paradoxical relationship of appearance to reality, of words to their meanings, or of experience to truth. In the *General Prologue* of the *Canterbury Tales*, Pilgrim Chaucer, the Narrator, presents a number of other pilgrims described in detail as to their social rank, habits, and even dress, each of whom, we are informed, will tell a couple of tales on their way to Canterbury and back, and in the entertaining process, probably reveal something of his or her own experience and peculiarities. This is a simple technique to prepare the audience for what it is about to hear. In fact, it is borrowed directly from an extensive and ancient literary tradition of the "framed story," used in Chaucer's own century by Boccaccio and Gower, among others.[19] Being accustomed to this genre, Chaucer's audience would know what to expect. However, in Chaucer's hands, as is usually the case, something borrowed becomes something new and greater—the *Canterbury Tales* becomes the epitome of the frame story.

The way in which the *Canterbury Tales* is constructed is the result of Chaucer's long preoccupation and experimentation with narrative structure. Given the nature of the man, one suspects that this concern has as much to do with philosophical inquiry as with merely developing craftsmanship. As John Gardner has suggested, Chaucer seems to have been intrigued by the implications of the nominalist debate for the validity of poetry.[20]

The Scholastics had labored long and hard to synthesize faith and reason by promoting the efficacy of reason far beyond anything anticipated before them. For Thomas Aquinas, not only are there universals, but the structure of the human mind is such that it can come to know them, as well as the structure of its own nature, and, to a more limited degree, God himself. Knowledge of the truth is attainable, albeit highly complex, and that knowledge is entirely communicable, preferably, for Saint Thomas, through logical discourse, but also through art in its mimetic function.[21]

In the *Canterbury Tales* there are various storytellers (or "authors") each trying to communicate a bit of truth, or perhaps even a bit of falsehood, to an audience. The first we meet is Chaucer the Pilgrim who introduces us to a whole series of other authors who will speak to us. Pilgrim Chaucer's position as author is privileged in that it is through his view that the other stories are filtered. Harry Bailly's position is special, too, since, although he himself tells no tale, he organizes, judges, and comments on the tales we hear. And then come the individual pilgrims.

While all of these are authors of individual stories, they are also, like the characters they create, fictional characters in an increasingly longer story, that of the *Canterbury Tales*. And so Chaucer seems to have created levels of characters. There is the level of Narrator who, through his reportage of the Canterbury frame story, creates pilgrims, like the Knight, who, in turn, become authors and create a third level of character in their tales, such as the character of Theseus. And there is still another dimension. The very authors who tell these stories are the audience for them on the way to Canterbury, and there is another audience beyond them in the person of the Host who must initiate, criticize, and judge, and still another audience, Chaucer the Narrator, who must listen closely both to the pilgrim authors and to Harry Bailly and do his best to report their tales. Is there still another level of audience? Of course there is. Splendidly hidden in all of this in God-like fashion is Geoffrey Chaucer the ultimate author of the *Canterbury Tales*, revealed in his fictional namesake and communicating, through this complicated structure, with us, the ultimate audience, hidden away, like the ultimate author, in the real world.

The effect of this complicated set of analogous audiences is to associate us as audience, at various times, with one or another of these fictional audiences within the poem. But our task, we begin to glean, is to get as close as we can to this ultimate author—to transcend fiction through fiction. Such a device brings us to the heart of Chaucer's poetics, in which the artist is first of all an audience, interpreting the ultimate text of reality itself and attempting to approach the intention of the ultimate, Divine Author as fully as possible. The true poet then reinvents or even translates his interpretation of that text into his poetic fiction, addressed to another audience, which will repeat his process of understanding in order to become authors. In this way, poetry becomes a paradigm for understanding.

This cosmological sense of Chaucerian construction becomes clearer when represented visually. There are usually seven spheres of authorship and/or audienceship in the *Canterbury Tales* (see figure 1).

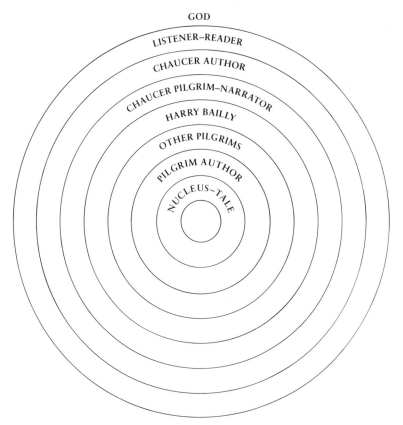

GOD
LISTENER–READER
CHAUCER AUTHOR
CHAUCER PILGRIM–NARRATOR
HARRY BAILLY
OTHER PILGRIMS
PILGRIM AUTHOR
NUCLEUS–TALE

Figure 1

For example, if the Wife of Bath were telling her tale, she would occupy the seventh sphere, while her tale of the hag and the rapacious
knight would occupy the nucleus, or core, of this cosmos. As one can
readily see, in a very real cosmic sense, God, the Ultimate Author and
Creator, occupies the first sphere, and it is also God who acts as the
Ultimate Audience and Judge, of the life-stories of the Canterbury pilgrims. The controlling analogy of the *Canterbury Tales,* then, is that
of the dynamics of fiction to the dynamics of existential reality.

If we are like the pilgrims in being an audience, which we surely are,
we are then, perhaps, also analogous to them in being authors. But we
have an advantage over the pilgrims, including Pilgrim Chaucer, in

that we may observe and learn their reactions to the stories and perceive their errors of interpretation, the stupidity and bad faith or, conversely, the humility and honesty that make for bad and good interpretation, good and bad authorship. The Canterbury pilgrims are on a fictional journey during which they act as audience and as authors, but that journey is firmly established as a large symbol for the pilgrimage of life. The structure of the *Canterbury Tales* is such that we as audience see ourselves as the final level of a whole series of flawed audiences. As soon as we do, we are lured into recognizing ourselves by analogy as the ultimate level of a whole series of flawed authors.

What is our story? When will the Host ask us to tell it? We have all been creating our stories from the beginning, even before we opened the *Canterbury Tales*, in the personal history each of us concocts for himself, or herself, because that is what life is, a happy or sad tale, a good or a bad story that we keep writing ourselves into. With Chaucer, we get to tell our story the moment we begin to act as audience to the other pilgrims, for interpreting another's story and creating your own are each part of the same activity.

There are probably few writers as didactic as Chaucer, and even fewer as subtle and successful at it. How well we will tell our tales depends upon how sensitively and intelligently we have listened to the other tales and profited from the examples of weakness and strength, hatred and love, honesty and dishonesty that have been shown us. In the same sense that Chaucer sets up this dialectic, we know that while in the world of fiction Harry Bailly will award only one pilgrim a prize for the best story, at Chaucer's own level of authorship and ours, there will be as many authors at the supper as there are well-wrought tales. We shall now examine some of those tales together with their authors and audiences.

· 5 ·

The General Prologue

The beautiful opening lines of the *General Prologue* provide for this little pilgrimage in time and space—the little space between London and Canterbury, the relatively short time needed to traverse it—a fully cosmic setting. Chaucer describes in the first eighteen lines the reawakening after winter of all nature's realm. Sweet rain relieves the dryness of dead earth, and flowers—the vegetative realm—come to life; the west wind, Zephirus, breathes life into plants; and the sun, in a zodiacal position of renewal, awakens the sleeping birds to their song of life and to procreation. We see the arrangement of the first few lines as hierarchical, the reawakening of nature at increasingly higher levels of life: plant, animal, and finally human. The author has also structured the lines so as to include in this vision of awakening the four constitutive elements of life: earth (the dry land), water (Aprill shoures), air (Zephirus), and fire (the yonge sonne).

> Whan that Aprill with his shoures soote [sweet showers]
> The droghte [dryness] of March hath perced to the roote,
> And bathed every veyne in swich licour [moistness]
> Of which vertu engendred is the flour;
> Whan Zephirus eek with his sweete breeth
> Inspired [blown into] hath in every holt [woods] and heeth
> The tendre croppes, and the yonge sonne
> Hath in the Ram his halve cours [course] yronne [run],
> And smale foweles [birds] maken melodye,
> That slepen al the nyght with open ye [eye]
> (So priketh [urges] hem nature in hir corages);
> Thanne longen folk to goon on pilgrimages,
> And palmeres for to seken straunge strondes,
> To ferne halwes [distant shrines], kowthe [known] in sondry
>   londes;

And specially from every shires ende
Of Engelond to Caunterbury they wende.
(1–16)

The entire hierarchy of the cosmos, as the Middle Ages had inherited it from Plato, is the setting for human renewal as symbolized by the pilgrimage to Canterbury. Chaucer places man at the center of this cosmos, as we see in the lines themselves, which are constructed so as to move toward and emphasize human reawakening as the center of this process:

WHEN (April showers quicken life on the vegetative level) (line 1)
↓
WHEN (nature inspires singing and mating on the animal level) (line 5)
↓
THEN (pilgrimages are made by renewed humanity) (line 12)

This simple device of rhetorical emphasis makes of man and, in the rest of the poem, of the whole pilgrimage, a microcosm, or little world, reflecting the structure and dynamics of the larger universe, the great macrocosm, God's creation with man at the center. The Middle Ages made good use of this idea that man and the universe were reflections of each other—in studying the nature of man to discover the structure of the cosmos and in contemplating the cosmic laws to discover the nature of man.

Even on first reading of these lines, the careful reader notices that while there is a hierarchical progress through nature to humanity and that while analogies are made from plant, to animal, to man, human nature is described differently: whereas the plants and animals only come to life, as they should, in a natural physical manner, blooming and being physically fertile, man's rebirth is signified by a spiritual impulse, which is natural to man: "Thanne longen folk to goon on pilgrimages" (12). Man, of course, possesses a nature that is both physical and spiritual, and by managing his lines this way Chaucer tells us that man's higher nature, while in harmony with the physical world, demands of him a spiritual reawakening. And so Chaucer prepares us through the symbol of the pilgrimage of life to witness in this Canterbury pilgrimage the spiritual reawakening and spiritual progress of these travelers. Again, the audience knows just what to expect.

The *Prologue* introduces Pilgrim Chaucer, the Narrator, who introduces twenty-nine figures assembled at the Tabard Inn in Southwerk preparing for their departure. Pilgrim Chaucer joins the company as does the Innkeeper, Harry Bailly, who proposes the storytelling contest and, with the assent of all, appoints himself guide and leader of the journey, as well as judge of the contest. He also proposes the prize for the winner: a meal paid for by all the other pilgrims—at Harry Bailly's Inn! Pilgrim Chaucer, who introduces himself as a figure within the general fiction of the *Canterbury Tales,* proceeds to introduce each of the other figures who will tell a tale, but just before doing so, he offers a rather unusual comment on his own literary method:

> But nathelees, whil I have tyme and space,
> Er that I ferther in this tale pace,
> Me thynketh it acordaunt to resoun
> To telle yow al the condicioun
> Of ech of hem, so as it semed me,
> And whiche they weren, and of what degree,
> And eek in what array that they were inne;
> And at a knyght than wol I first bigynne.
> (35–42)

Chaucer gives us here something more than the conventional medieval rhetorical criteria for storytelling, although spelling out even those would be unusual. He invokes reason as his poetic criterion, which leads him to present "the condicioun," that is, not only the pilgrims' worldly circumstances, but also their dispositions, character, behavior, and very mode of being. Chaucer intends, as we shall see later, to present the social, psychological, and spiritual states of the figures he describes. This "resounable" process is reinforced and expanded by the narrator's addition of "degree" as another of his descriptive goals. Again we will discover through Pilgrim Chaucer's words the social rank, the moral development, and the spiritual progress, or lack thereof, that each of the pilgrims has achieved, or failed to achieve, in his or her journey through life. And, finally, he will tell us what they looked like.

The "resounable" procedure, or better, rational poetics, is, however, qualified by the inclusion of the Narrator's disclaimer, "so as it semed me" (as it seemed or appeared to be to me, as best I can). The *ratio* of reasonable poetry, then, would seem to depend on the intellectual condition of the poet himself, on his ability to know, and so the audience has every right to inquire into it. As it happens, Chaucer gives us plenty of material by which to assess the trustworthiness of the narrator. But making good sense of poetry also depends on the audience, and Chaucer's medieval audience would certainly have remembered from his earlier poem *Troilus and Criseyde* what he expected of his listeners and readers—the ability to come to the poetry with intelligence and good will: "Now herkneth with a good entencioun" (52). The rationality of poetry, then, like any other use of reason to discover the truth, has certain limitations including the poet's skill and good intention and the audience's intelligence and good intention. As with every other author and audience, a certain contract exists here between the two. In the case of Chaucer, as we see from the line of *Troilus and Criseyde* above, the terms of the contract are specific.[22] Even with such a mutual understanding, both author and audience are constrained by the limits of language, not only in describing appearances but also in revealing the true relationship between appearance and reality.

Pilgrim Chaucer starts off true to his promise to be reasonable, for he begins his description with the Knight, reflecting the same tendency toward hierarchy as in the first eighteen lines. The Knight is the highest figure in the social hierarchy of the *Canterbury Tales*, and since in the Middle Ages recognition of order and the ordering function is preeminently reasonable, Chaucer, in beginning with the Knight, has already begun to reflect the complex medieval concept of "resoun." When later the tale-telling actually begins, we see that the order of reason is respected not only voluntarily by pilgrims who so opt, but also by fortune and nature, since in the drawing of straws to see who will begin, the victory of the Knight preserves the decorum of natural, as well as social, order.

The narrator's presentation of the Knight also seems to correspond to the artistic principles he has laid down. His description falls into three parts, as do, by and large, all the descriptions: his virtues, his behavior, and his physical appearance. His virtues are presented first and emphasized, for he is, within his limits, truly virtuous. His are active virtues, and his long list of military accomplishments is harmonious with the virile qualities ascribed to him: valor, faithfulness, honor, generosity, and gentility. After listing his many victories, the narrator returns to his virtues and summarizes them thus: "And though that he were worthy, he was wys [wise], / And of his port [behavior] as meeke as is a mayde" (68–69). The Knight is specified as not only a good soldier but as a model of the reasonable man, combining in a proper harmony the male (*vir*) virtues (*virtus*) of courage and wisdom with the female virtues of mercy and prudence. Thus the Knight embodies balance.

If we turn for a moment to the *Knight's Tale*, we shall see another of Chaucer's techniques: the tales not only confirm or demonstrate aspects of the teller's character, appearance, and personality as revealed in the *General Prologue*, but they expand and add to that portrait.

One of Chaucer's great achievements, the *Knight's Tale*[23] has roots going back to Virgil and Statius, but Chaucer's immediate source is Boccaccio's *Il Teseido*. In Chaucer's hands, however, what was a rather turgid recitation becomes a masterpiece of medieval literature. He enriches the tale with generous doses of the philosophical thought of Boethius, and develops or changes character, description, and action. For example, in Boccaccio's original, Arcita perishes when he crushes his chest; Chaucer has Arcite fall on his head—a crucial change. The result is a glittering, entertaining, and thought-provoking romance.

Like most of the *Canterbury Tales*, the *Knight's Tale* contains in it its author as character. Theseus, the ruler and authority, is a pagan embodiment of the Canterbury Knight himself, representing the rule of reason over appetite both in his personal psyche and in the political world. His subjugation of the Amazons, appetite ruling reason, and his wedding of their queen, Ypolita, signify a restoration in the public realm of harmonious rule and in the psychological realm of proper order, exactly paralleled in the Narrator's description of the Knight himself. The conventional use in the Middle Ages of female to represent appetite and male to represent reason was intended as an analysis of the human psyche, not as sociology or sexism. The ideal healthy human psyche harmoniously combined both appetite and reason, both male and female dimensions. Thus the Canterbury Knight is both virile and "meeke as is a mayde" (69), and so Theseus, wedding himself to the Amazon, or female principle, becomes complete. It is this same harmony of reason and desire that must be achieved by the young knights, Palamon and Arcite, in their relationship with Theseus (just authority), with themselves (moral authority), and with the beautiful Emelye (authority of nature). In Theseus's "First Mover" speech at the marriage of Palamon and Emelye, the destruction and disorder that have been created by the irrational pursuit of the good are repaired and restored in harmony with the Neoplatonic "faire cheyne of love" (*Knight's Tale*, 2988). Thus the Canterbury audience has had set for it a proper and orthodox philosophical structure to follow in their tales.

Had all the succeeding tales been variations on the large philosophical ethos provided by the Knight, the Narrator would have been faithful to his aesthetic of presenting reasonable authors telling rational stories, and thus to his definition of poetry as "resoun," likely at the risk of boring us all thoroughly. But as old Egeus in the *Knight's Tale* has declared, in two lines that have become among Chaucer's best known: "This world nys but a thurghfare ful of wo, / And we been pilgrymes, passynge to and fro" (2847–48). Poetry exists within life and time and Chaucer seems to have accepted this limitation at the outset of the poem: "whil I have tyme and space" (35). Thus the Canterbury pilgrimage must have its share of woe and must experience the failure of the ideal, which causes such woe. Chaucer's pilgrims, like life's, do not pursue an undeterred progress, advancing each at the same speed toward the pilgrimage's goal; as in life, they go forward and backward.

We begin to see signs of this even as Chaucer the Pilgrim continues his description of his fellow travelers in the *General Prologue*. When he gets to the Prioress, for instance, his method of description subtly changes. Her depiction begins not with any reference to virtues, as in the presentation of the Knight, but rather with a combination of physical characteristics and petty mannerisms. Her smile, simple and coy, is what we first see, and it is with this ambiguous smile that she will tell her tale, a startling combination of intellectual simplicity and moral coyness. Her singing, her French pronunciation, her table manners and social pretensions, are all described before Chaucer—almost as an afterthought—adds, "But, for to speken of hire conscience" (142). The Narrator has almost forgotten to tell us of her virtues, and that, of course, tells all: the Prioress's moral life is meager and limited. It needs only nine of the forty-five lines of her description to exhaust her ethical range, and this woman from whom the audience will later hear a tale in which human beings, with the full approval of the author of the tale, are drawn by horses and hanged, nevertheless weeps when she sees a mouse caught in a trap and when her lap dogs are kicked or abused. As the Narrator says, "And al was conscience and tendre herte" (150).

The Prioress's description is a study in smallness: her mouth is small and red, she keeps small dogs, her mannerisms are minute, her bracelet, "smal." This is counterbalanced by her broad forehead, a sign in the Middle Ages of stupidity, and Chaucer suggests that she was a chubby little person: "For, hardily, she was nat undergrowe" (156). The cumulative picture is one of a Kewpie doll who in her tale extends and fulfills the study in physical tinyness by revealing a concomitant moral smallness that is the atrophy of the human spirit.

The last detail of her appearance that we are given is that of the coral bracelet she wears, on which is written the motto "*Amor vincit omnia*." The audience is then allowed to see whether love conquers all in her anti-Semitic tale, told, she claims, with the innocence of "a child of twelf month oold, or lesse" (*Prioress's Prologue*, 484), in which love has degenerated into sentimentality, with its inevitable offspring, loathing and brutality.

It is in this description that the audience might begin to question the judgment of Pilgrim Chaucer, the Narrator. He seems to approve of the Prioress, finds her amiable, and has nothing but praise for her comportment. The irony we perceive in her description is produced by a kind of flash of communication we get with Chaucer the Author over the head of Pilgrim Chaucer. The author catches our eye, so to speak, and winks. That's an important wink because it essentially undermines the authority of the Narrator and puts us on guard. Can we trust him? Well, we have to, at least to a certain extent, but from now on we realize that things are not quite what they seem to be. Monks, for instance! The medieval expectations for this order of clergy included prayer, fasting, manual labor, and mediation, but our narrator introduces us to quite another sort, and he approves of him heartily. The description of the Canterbury Monk is one composed of contradictions. The Narrator depicts him as a "manly man" whose chief interest in life is hunting. The Monk has no enthusiasm whatsoever for the monastic rule or any other guide that would so regulate his life as to make him be what he appears to be. The same irony that is present in the Prioress's description is present here, but Chaucer communicates it to us over the head of the narrator in a slightly different way.

The Monk is said to love *venerie*, a word which in this context means "hunting," but which is akin to, and suggestive of, *venery*, "sexual pleasure," derived from the name and idea of Venus. Indeed, in the Middle Ages, a euphemism for the pursuit of fornication was "the hunt of Venus." The bells on the Monk's bridle are described as ringing every bit as loudly as the bells of the chapel, and this contrast of the two kinds of bells refers the audience back to a well-known symbolic tradition. Medieval art often depicted a crowned figure playing a set of bells graduated in size. The figure represented the harmony of reason, since these bells, struck according to a mathematical formula, produced harmonious sound. Behind the visual representation lay a scriptural tradition, that of King David whose Psalms were considered an example of great wisdom produced by reason. This employment of a visual scene or picture to communicate a poetic idea is called iconography, and Chaucer was a master of it.[24]

The competing bells of the Monk's bridle are not graduated but are all the same size, like sleigh bells. They cannot produce harmony, but rather jangle with a cacophonous sound. It is to this irrational jangling rather than to the sound of harmonious reason that the Monk gallops on his "venerial" ride. His rejection of the life of the mind is explicit, and the narrator agrees: "And I seyde his opinion was good. / What sholde he studie and make hymselven wood [mad]" (183–84), and Chaucer winks again. The Monk opts for the hunt: "Of prikyng and of huntyng for the hare / Was al his lust, for no cost wolde he spare" (191–92). Hunting for rabbits hardly seems much of a challenge for a "manly man," one as robust as our Monk, but the narrator sees no inappropriateness. Chaucer's specification of the hunt as having the hare as its goal suggest another iconographic tradition, already mentioned, that of the hunt of Venus which had as its prey "a small furry creature,"[25] and with this allusion the ironic description of the Monk as a sexual predator is reemphasized.

The Monk's appearance is richly described; he wears a fur-trimmed coat and a golden pin under his hood, which appropriately enough is shaped like a "love-knotte." His face is gleaming as if it were oiled, and his eyes bulge and blaze as if on fire. Such peculiar physical characteristics Chaucer seems to have taken from the medieval sciences of medicine and physiognomy, in which they indicate an alarming moral and physical condition.

This deceptive figure continues his deceit when it comes time to tell his tale. Our Host, Harry Bailly, taunts the Monk as he invites him to tell his story, perceiving, unlike the narrator, the shameful difference between what he is and what he ought to be. "You're in pretty good shape for one who lives the hard life of a monk," teases Bailly. "It's a shame you're a monk and have to deny yourself women; you'd improve the race immensely with the results of your lust." From the Host's later words of assurance that he is only kidding, we imagine that he has produced a flush of anger in the Monk, but he cannot resist adding the taunt that there is often much truth in jest.

As if to disprove the Host's depiction of him as an ignorant sensualist, the Monk goes on to tell a sententious and boring tale, introduced in a pretentiously learned manner, in which he lists the falls of great figures in history, from Lucifer to Croesus of Lydia. It is the Knight who finally orders an end to the tale, unable to listen to one more tedious tragedy. If, as we begin to suspect, the motivation for the story was to get vengeance on the Host for having unmasked him, and to restore his dignity, then the Monk has achieved one of his ends, for Harry is thoroughly bored and irritated.[26] The Host refers again to the bridle bells, which, he says, are the only thing that kept him awake as they accompanied the tale. He reminds the Monk of the wise clerk's saying that no matter how significant the meaning of a tale, it is worth nothing if there is no audience to hear it, and we wonder whether or not it is Author Chaucer speaking through his character. But here, perhaps, it is Harry who has missed the point, for it seems that the tale of this Monk is as empty and meaningless as is his practice of his profession. Rather its intent was to reconstruct the facade of respectability, which permits his hunting game. Such would seem to be his reply to Harry's invitation to tell another tale more in keeping with his character, perhaps something about hunting: " 'Nay,' quod this Monk, 'I have no lust to pleye.' " (*Prologue of the Nun's Priest's Tale*, 2806).

In contrast to the corrupt Monk, the *General Prologue* presents another cleric, the Parson, who is the epitome of simple virtue, a credit to his profession and a witness to man's moral perfectibility. The Narrator lists his virtues with an unusual reverence, and the complete absence of irony suggests that for once, at least, Pilgrim Chaucer and Chaucer the Author see things in exactly the same way. The Parson's spiritual life is, in fact, so rich that the Narrator provides no description of his appearance at all, a rare and, perhaps, significant departure from his usual descriptive method. This pilgrim, we are told, is poor in worldly goods but rich in good works. Nor is he a simple innocent, but rather, he is "also a lerned man, a clerk, / That Cristes gospel trewely wolde preche" (480–81). The center of his virtue is the principle that first one practices the good and afterward teaches it; that is, you teach and preach what you are. This lesson he has learned most likely from his study of Scripture, for instance, Matthew 5.19, and as well from his reading of Augustine, where he would have found the idea that to know the good truly is to love it, and that no one who does not love the good can really possess it. This leads Augustine to the view that the good man and the speaker of the truth are always one and the same. There was, however, disagreement about this assertion even in the Middle Ages, and Thomas Aquinas declared in contrast that goodness was a matter of will, not intellect, and that a corrupt will and correct intellect could coexist in the same man. In other words, one could know the truth and yet speak falseness and evil.

The Parson would seem to depict the Augustinian principle of "the good man skilled in speaking," for he is explicitly said to be both learned and virtuous. But other pilgrims differ. Some possess neither virtue nor skill, but several tell effective and convincing tales despite, or perhaps because of, their moral corruption. Another cleric whom we will look at in some detail even articulates the opposing position as an introduction to his story, confessing himself to be completely depraved but able to teach virtue to others. Chaucer obviously found this debate interesting and important to the delineation of the Pardoner, and as we shall see, the idea becomes central to the Pilgrim-Author's poetics.

Interestingly enough, Chaucer assigns the Parson a tale that by anyone's judgment would hardly win the literary prize. It may be meant to knit up and conclude the *Canterbury Tales*, as both the Host and the Parson indicate, and is therefore solemn and serious, told in prose, not poetry, in order to eschew all decoration and elaboration of language. It is also noteworthy that Pilgrim Chaucer resorts to prose in his own tale as well, but for different and comic reasons. The use of prose in these two strategically important tales is itself significant, for it alludes to a concern seen throughout the *Canterbury Tales*—that of the relation of language to truth, and, more specifically, of different forms of expression to meaning. The Parson explains his rejection of fables by referring to Saint Paul, who says: "For the time shall come when they will not endure sound doctrine; but after their own lusts they shall heap to themselves teachers, having itching ears; And they shall turn away their ears from the truth, and shall be turned unto fables" (2 Tim. 4.3–4). The Parson ascribes to a theory, discussed above and further below, in which language has a real and inherent relationship to truth, and he, therefore, makes the important distinction between poetic language (fiction) and prose (analytic language). Lacking rhetorical skills and uneasy about the ways of manipulating language, he chooses prose. His creator gives much evidence of being equally concerned about this question, but Chaucer chooses to explore language in all its modes in order to get to the bottom of it. The Parson's rejection of poetry, the mode of fiction and fables, may be based on his experience of listening to so many of the pilgrims abusing poetic language in their stories. Be that as it may, his own tale fails to solve the problem of language because it essentially eschews language in its more complex modes. While he certainly instructs, he can hardly be said to delight, and his contribution must be taken as only one element in the answer to the question of fiction's seriousness and value.

The Parson takes the precaution to inquire into his audience's willingness to listen attentively to his kind of story, and he finds the Canterbury pilgrims in a serious mood. The Narrator specifies that the pilgrims informed the Host of their willingness to accept the terms that the Parson had laid down, and with this audience-author contract the Parson begins his long sermon on penance, in which, with patience, the reader can find a description of many of the vices and shortcomings that have been seen in each of the pilgrims through their tales.

A few further examples may be given of Chaucer's method of linking the figures described in the *General Prologue* to the tales these authors tell.

The Merchant plunges directly into the famous "marriage debate" of the *Canterbury Tales* with the enthusiasm and lack of caution of the partisan. His tale is told directly after the Clerk's, whose theme has been the great virtue and steadfastness of the heroine, Griselde, in the trials she experienced in marriage. The *Merchant's Tale*, as if in answer to the Clerk's, presents the trials and sufferings of a husband in marriage, but it goes wildly astray and is hardly an appropriate response to the ideas raised in the *Clerk's Tale*. It becomes, in the seemingly autonomous process of fiction, a statement quite other than that intended by its author and one that goes well beyond the specific theme of marriage.

In the *General Prologue*, the Narrator presents the Merchant as a rich and imposing figure. He is apparently an international trader with dealings on the Continent. The brief portrait of the Merchant in the *General Prologue* hints that his business included dishonest and even criminal dealings, and this element suggests a contradiction in the figure himself. While on the one hand he is described as solemn, worthy, and stately, on the other hand he is also a thoroughgoing materialist, deceitful, and totally dedicated to profit making. Another important feature of his description in the *General Prologue* is the juxtaposition of what is revealed and what is concealed. The Merchant is constantly revealing his ability to multiply profits ("Sownynge [revealing] alwey th'encrees of his wynnyng" [275]) while concealing debts ("Ther wiste no wight [no one knew] that he was in dette" [280]). The Narrator concludes the description of this wheeler-dealer, "With his bargaynes and with his chevyssaunce [dealing for profit]" (282), with the unusual but significant remark that the Merchant's name was not known to him.

This same dynamic of revealing and concealing runs throughout the *Merchant's Tale* and emerges as its very theme, with extensions that include seeing and blindness, knowing and ignorance, fact and fancy. Finally, it is a tale the very subject of which is fiction and truth and the ability, or inability, to distinguish between them. It is introduced by its author in a highly biographical way—as a further contribution to the subject of the relations of men and women in marriage. Like the *Wife of Bath's Tale*, it is specified as having its origin in the personal experience of the author, who, we are told, has been married only two months and has discovered already the innumerable torments a woman will inflict upon a man.

As in several of the pilgrims' presentations, then, the context of the *Merchant's Tale* is infused with a great degree of realism. But it is finally the biography of a nameless man, a figure who appears to be one thing but is something else, revealed and concealed simultaneously. As the audience perceives this, it also perceives something of the complicated nature of fiction and, indeed, of reality, or fact, and, ultimately, the relation between the two.

The tale itself, presented by the Merchant after his biographical and "realistic" introduction, abandons realism altogether, being set in times gone by, employing a quite unlikely plot, and introducing mythological actors and actresses. The Merchant's intention, however, is to enable his audience to apply the meaning of his parable to their own lives, which, as we see at the end of the tale, is exactly what Harry Bailly does. However, as in so many of Chaucer's tales, the theme of the story of January and May frees itself from the author's personal intention, and what the author wished to reveal turns out to be secondary while what was concealed becomes the real content of the tale.

The story told by the Merchant is Chaucer's particularly brilliant rendition of the ancient "*senex amans*" theme. The subject of the old man who marries a young wife was a favorite of poets and moralists alike long before the time of Chaucer and after. The theme allowed the exploration of a number of juxtaposed ideas—youth and age, wisdom and folly, and, in general, the idea of the combination of opposites—all under a metaphoric guise of an old man led into error by his desire for a young and too vigorous girl. Thus the Merchant introduces us to a "worthy" knight allegorically named January, suggesting winter, and May, the young woman he marries, whose name suggests, of course, spring. By nature's laws, winter and spring occur separately and are not combined, and the unnaturalness of the old knight's choice of mate is thus suggested.

In fulfillment of the author's intention to show the perfidy of women, the plot centers on May's successful scheme to betray her husband with a young man. But before the central event, the audience has already perceived January as a sententious, self-deluded, and self-serving old fool.

We see this particularly clearly when January seeks the advice of two counselors, Placebo (I will please), a false counselor, and Justinus (just, correct), a true counselor, on the question of whether he should marry a young wife. Placebo essentially tells January what he wants to hear and, indeed, repeats to him what January himself has just finished saying. Justinus, quoting Seneca, advises January to seek a wife who is a person of virtue, intelligence, and goodwill rather than to seek a sensually delectable mate. January, however, is deaf to good advice, and this inability to perceive the truth is presented through the image of blindness: "For love is blynd alday, and may nat see" (*Merchant's Tale*, 1598). January's first blindness, then, is metaphoric and occurs while he is still physically clear-sighted. Later he will actually lose his vision, providing May her opportunity to dupe him, but he will be no more blind intellectually and morally than he is in the earlier scene, where he is already blinded by lust. January does not see what is plainly revealed to him, but he sees what in reality does not exist, his passionate fantasy of the ideal wife: "He purtreyed [pictured] in his herte and in his thoght / Hir fresshe beautee and hir age tendre, / Hir myddel [waist] smal, hire armes longe and sklendre [slender]" (1600–1602). Like Pygmalion, January gives shape and reality to his cupidinous imaginings and falls in love with his own fiction.

In a final effort to steer his friend from disaster, Justinus advises January that if he must marry a young woman, he should at least behave reasonably and moderately with her, and then, in a masterful touch of wit, the Pilgrim-Author has Justinus conclude his advice by telling January that if he had been listening carefully when the Wife of Bath told her tale ("The Wyf of Bathe, if ye han understonde . . .") he would need no further proof of the woe that is in marriage. Suddenly at this line (1685), the questions of who is audience, who character, who author become paramount. Chaucer has reminded us once again, right in the middle of a fictitious tale, that we must try to keep straight the lines between fiction and the real. They can, we see, so easily become confused.

January has certainly confused them in his ridiculous fiction about his own physical vigor, as well as May's delight in it. So taken is he with the fleshly delights of marriage, that he creates a walled garden, a paradise on earth, in which he makes love all day long. Into this paradise creeps misfortune. January is suddenly stricken blind. His moral blindness is now completed by physical blindness, which conceals from him the sight of his beautiful but faithless wife. Since he cannot now possess and control his bride by watching, he resorts to holding onto her hand day and night.

Anguished by this increased imprisonment, May decides to use January's blindness to her own advantage. Having arranged to have the squire Damyan, the youth she really loves, hidden in the branches of a fruit tree in the garden, May convinces her blind husband to boost her into the tree on the pretext of her hunger for its fruit. In the midst of May and Damyan's lovemaking in the tree, January's sight is restored and he sees the couple mating in the tree "In swich manere [in such a way that] it may nat been expressed" (2362).

January at last sees things as they really are, and the dangers of his marriage to a young woman, earlier revealed by Justinus but concealed by his own lustful foolishness, are now revealed as clearly and brutally as possible. He moves from moral blindness to physical blindness to physical sight, and we, the audience, fully expect that, chastised as he is by reality, he will now achieve moral insight as well. But such is not to be, for May has been given a very special gift, that of language. We see the guilty wife use language to represent what her husband has seen with his own eyes in such a way as to convince him that he has totally misunderstood what he witnessed; indeed, that he has not seen what he has seen.

January is happy once again, having rejected what was revealed and settled back into the comfort of his inner blindness, secure in the reality created by May's clever use of words.

May redescribes the scene in the pear tree witnessed by her husband in language aimed at suspension of disbelief. January, as the audience to this verbal re-creation, is first skeptical: "He swyved [had sex with] thee, I saugh it with myne yen [eyes]" (2378). But the power of fiction is such that January eventually seeks May's pardon for his ill-mannered suspicions and returns to the bliss of his moral blindness, rejecting the reality that has been revealed to him. As May says, many a man thinks he has seen a thing which is in reality quite otherwise.

But language does not always work for the author's intention. Certainly the Merchant feels that his fiction has convincingly presented the reality he wishes to propound: that women are treacherous and the bane of a man's existence. Although he has certainly convinced the Host that the content of his tale is only its surface, the Merchant, concealer though he is, reveals more than he intends. The larger audience progressively penetrates the allegory of the tale to discover that January, and not May, is the author of his misfortune, and in doing so, the audience discovers something more about the nature of fiction and of interpretation.

Another member of the middle class participating in the pilgrimage is the Franklin, a wealthy landowner whose position in medieval society was apparently high, but somewhat short of aristocratic. The description of him in the *General Prologue* is one marked by richness and plentitude, centering on the table and food. His show of riches, particularly in the ability to receive guests elegantly and expensively, suggests his desire to appear lordly in his way of life. This same inordinate concern is seen in the Franklin's prologue and after in his tale. We first encounter him directly when he reacts to the the tale the Squire tells with exaggerated praise and embarrassing deference to this young, and rather frivolous, aristocrat.

In the social aspect of his portrait, we see the Franklin as a nouveau riche, a person recently risen from a lower class due solely to financial success, who attempts to deny and camouflage his roots and convince himself and others of his inherent nobility by acquiring and displaying what he perceives are the accoutrements and accomplishments of his new class. In the Franklin's case, food and language are the signs he has chosen to signify a truth that is nonexistent. In his own peculiar way the Franklin subscribes to the theory that you are what you eat: "Withoute bake mete [food] was nevere his hous / Of fissh and flessh, and that so plentevous, / It snewed [snowed] in his hous of mete and drynke" (343–45).

In having on his table and in consuming the same foods that sustain the aristocrat, the Franklin feels that he approaches true nobility. That the definition of nobility this implies is shallow and meaningless goes unnoticed by the Franklin, who is so absorbed in outer signs that he has little time for inner realities, and thus the tale he tells in order to lay claim to natural nobility backfires on him by exposing his vulgarity of mind and manners.

In his praise of the Squire's tale, the Franklin, although addressing the youth directly, is really speaking through him to the Knight, for by flattery of the son he hopes to compliment the father and win his approbation. His praise concentrates on the sophistication of the language used by the Squire in his tale, the union of wit and feeling, his eloquence, and discretion. He is, in other words, delighted by style and knows quite well that style of speech, not content, is the principal sign by which many an audience judges a speaker. But the Franklin has inverted even this process, because it is not the Squire's speech that leads him to identify the author's nobility, but rather, aware of the Squire's social status, the Franklin declares his language noble. The *Squire's Tale* is a highly conventional romance, incomplete and ill-constructed, and generally a rather tiresome affair. The Franklin himself tells a far superior tale and thus, we may suppose, is aware of his insincerity in praising his literary inferior.

But, typical of the pretentious, this Pilgrim-Author is full of false modesty and self-denigration. While praising the Squire for virtues he obviously does not possess, he belittles his own son publicly for unaristocratic vices, including that of preferring conversation with a page to conversation with gentlemen. The Franklin has broken off relations with his son, as if this ungenteel progeny were all that prevented him from being recognized for the aristocrat he feels he really is.

Harry Bailly is full of disdain for this kind of snobbishness and in typical fashion deflates the Franklin's puffery: "Straw for youre gentillesse!" he says scornfully here (*Squire's Tale*, 695). But as the Franklin thrives on rich sauces, so, too, does he thrive on the disdain of the likes of Bailly, and he condescendingly professes complete obedience to the Host, declaring haughtily that if only his tale is sufficiently well-wrought to please the Host's sensibilities, he will know he has achieved literary success. Did he then wink at the Knight? He is certainly impertinent enough to have done so, as his self-absorbed tale demonstrates.

Like his life, the Franklin's language is all tactics in the war on reality. Loathing himself, he attempts to create another self. Crucial to his effort to create signs of an aristocratic self is the central tactic of denigration of the actual self. Like the Merchant, the Franklin plays the game of concealing and revealing, being careful to conceal the self-created proofs of his personal worth in such a way that they are easily discovered by others. Thus he begins the prologue to his tale with the disclaimer that he is but a coarse man and must be excused for the rudeness of his speech. He knows no rhetoric, the Franklin claims, and goes on to describe his ignorance in the most rhetorical language: "I sleep nevere on the Mount of Pernaso [Mount Parnassus], / Ne lerned Marcus Tullius Scithero [Cicero]" (*Franklin's Prologue*, 721–22).

The Franklin's theory seems to be that the lower you cringe the higher you will be raised when the signs of your true worth—which you yourself create and conceal—are discovered by the truly noble who are able to recognize them. And thus his tale is one in which all kinds of false signs of nobility are employed to conceal the sign that the author really wishes to have recognized as the true sign of true nobility. In this way the Franklin's theory of psychology exactly parallels certain theories of rhetoric, particularly the idea that concealment of the truth by rhetorical figures increases the delight felt by the audience when it discovers what is hidden, and increases the value the audience attaches to what has been revealed.

His tale presents characters representative of the social class he aspires to, as well as a clerk who, like the author, is from the broad middle class. The Breton knight, Arveragus, has taken Dorigen as wife, and their relationship is based on mutual respect, mutual obedience, and love. This concept of the male-female relationship is based on the medieval theory of friendship and the equality that sustains it. The Franklin's description of Dorigen and Arveragus's marriage anchored in friendship appears then to emerge as the ideal answer to the

The Canterbury Tales

"marriage debate" that runs throughout the *Canterbury Tales*. But the Franklin introduces into his tale a further element intended to create a different theme, that of true nobility. The author manages this new theme in such a way as to undermine the ideal of human relations included in the tale. This he does by introducing a passionate squire, Aurelius, who has fallen in love with Dorigen and presses his suit during her husband's absence. To be rid of Aurelius's incessant entreaties for her love, Dorigen assigns the suitor an impossible task, the accomplishment of which, she pledges, will win him his desires.

The task itself is significant: to remove the cliffs that bind the coast of Brittany. Aurelius's challenge, therefore, is nothing less than the transformation of physical reality itself. The impossibility of the proposition is intended by Dorigen to express the impossibility of her love for anyone but her husband, Arveragus. She is to learn, however, that in the world of the Franklin, absolutes are unstable and appearances may be deformed in such a way as to deform reality itself.

Aurelius employs a clerk specializing in magic who, the text tells us, can make things appear to be what they are not. Aurelius agrees to pay the clerk a fortune to make the cliffs of Brittany disappear. The magician does little more than await the natural floods, which allow the sea to rise up and cover the rocks along the coast of Brittany. The moral predicament of the story now takes shape. Aurelius claims his reward by holding the noble Dorigen to her promise, and she is faced with the choice of betraying her marriage oath or breaking her word. Arveragus, faced with the dilemma of choosing between giving his wife to another man or bearing the disgrace of her breaking her word, comes down quickly on the side of the necessity of a noble person's keeping her word, although with much grief and weeping.

The Franklin interrupts the story at this point to urge us not to weep for Dorigen just yet, as a happier fate awaits her. This the author constructs by having Aurelius experience feelings of pity for the woman and admiration for the gentility of her husband. Wishing to appear still nobler than the noble knight, Arveragus, the squire, Aurelius, releases Dorigen from her promise and forgoes his pleasure. The Franklin draws the lesson for us: "Thus kan a squier doon a gentil dede /

As wel as kan a knyght, withouten drede" (1543–44). The author's intention, then, has been to show that those of a lower social status, a squire in this case, are capable of a degree of nobility equal to those of a higher social status, and he believes his tale has demonstrated this reductive proposition. But his intention is not yet totally fulfilled.

When Aurelius's debt to the clerk comes due, he complains that such a payment will require that he sell his entire heritage. Hearing the story of the squire's "nobility" in forgoing his lust, the clerk enters the competition to be most genteel:

> Thou art a squier, and he is a knyght;
> But God forbede, for his blisful myght,
> But if a clerk koude doon a gentil dede
> As wel as any of yow, it is no drede! (1609–12)

With considerable panache, the socially humble clerk forgives the wealthy squire his enormous debt entirely. "Have good day!" (1619), he says blithely, and gallops off on his horse. Now, that's class! Or so, at least, the author of the tale would like his audience to believe. The Franklin coyly concludes his tale by asking the audience to help him interpret its final meaning:

> Lordynges, this question, thanne, wol I aske now,
> Which was the mooste fre [liberal], as thynketh yow?
> Now telleth me, er that ye ferther wende [go].
> I kan [know] namoore; my tale is at an ende.
> (1621–24)

The Franklin has constructed his tale with great care so that his conclusion, that the least socially distinguished is the most noble, is inescapable. He desires that from his fiction will emerge a view of reality in which natural aristocracy achieved through virtue is superior to legal aristocracy achieved through accident of birth. And this view of reality will, he believes, fulfill his personal ambition to appear noble. Throughout the tale he has rhetorically concealed all the clues necessary to lead an audience to this view, much as the clerk has concealed the cliffs of Brittany by magic. His question of who is most noble is based on his sly understanding that the audience will be more thoroughly convinced of a truth that they believe they have themselves discovered than one forced upon them by the author.

But the most perceptive among the pilgrims and other audiences of the *Franklin's Tale* have already understood that the magician's concealing was a fraud and that despite appearances, under the water of the sea, the rocks remain, awaiting only nature's course to emerge and reassert their existence. Similarly, the false values of the Franklin do not become true through his fiction, but lurk beneath the oceans of his artful language to reemerge, like dangerous shoals, when the waves of his tale have subsided and the audience returns to the reality the author would transform.

Ironically, both the false and the true definition of real nobility are contained within the tale, for indeed true virtue is the basis of true nobility. But the author's desire for the appearance, rather than the substance, of nobility leads him to miss the redeeming truth of his own fiction.

While it is not possible to discuss each pilgrim's description in the *General Prologue*, and its relation to his or her tale, in those already discussed we have begun to see Chaucer's emphasis on the relation of author to tale. This emphasis, while contributing to a certain kind of realism on one level, is not, it seems, primarily aimed at psychological appropriateness, but rather at an exploration of how fiction gets made and what links it has to the real. Before examining in detail some of the fictional creations of the *Canterbury Tales*, a brief look at the Friar will be useful in clarifying Chaucer's use of the *General Prologue* to set the stage for the tales.

There is little doubt arising from the Narrator's description that we are to take the Friar as a corrupt and negative figure. The nature of his corruption as seen in the *General Prologue* is essentially moral, but in his tale and its prologue the Friar is also revealed as intellectually corrupt. The Friar is an interesting figure because he is linked in one way or another to so many of the other pilgrims: he is, we are told in the *General Prologue*, a companion of the Franklin because of his worldly interests; he attacks the Summoner in his own tale, and he speaks directly to the Wife of Bath's accomplishments as an author. The characteristics of the Friar noted by the Narrator in the *General Prologue* principally include materialism and lust, and these are seen, in part, in his attitude toward language. He knows "fair langage [language]" (211), we are told, and he has a special theory of signs by which he knows the true intention of penitents who confess to him. While prayer or weeping are for him inferior signs of regret, the giving of money he considers an infallible sign of true contrition (232). His own rhetorical abilities in preaching are used to produce the universal sign from even the poorest in his audiences. The Friar is concerned not only with the content of speech, but, we are told at last, he perfects its form by affecting a lisp "To make his Englissh sweete upon his tonge" (265).

Huberd, as the Friar is named, is thus much concerned with language and signs, and it is therefore not surprising that his tale is about such matters. His primary intention as author is to attack the Summoner, apparently because of traditional rivalries between their professions, and he states this intention openly in the prologue to his tale—so openly, in fact, that the Host is alarmed and warns the Friar to be careful. The summoner of Huberd's tale is an outright villain, the personification of lechery, greed, deception, and cruelty. In his travels collecting fines and monies, the summoner meets up with a figure who claims to be a bailiff, with whom, because of their common interests, he swears brotherhood. Only when the summoner has revealed to the bailiff all his vices in a confessional scene, does the figure reveal his true identity, and then only after clearly establishing that it is the summoner's true intention that he does so: "'Brother,' quod he, 'wiltow [do you wish] that I thee telle? / I am a feend [devil]; my dwellyng is in helle' " (*Friar's Tale*, 1447–48).

The summoner, far from being horrified to discover his brotherhood with a demon, is fascinated by the question of form and by the devil's ability to assume various appearances and to adapt and use various outward forms without possessing the substance of those forms. While the devil does his best to explain this shape-shifting power, he concludes by assuring the summoner that he will someday know the answer to the question by his own experience.

The brothers encounter two incidents on their travels that permit the devil to teach the summoner an ironic lesson about appearance and substance, sign and signified, and principally about language and intention. In the first, they observe a man struggling to force his cart from the mud. In his frustration the carter curses his horses, crying, "The devel have al, bothe hors and cart and hey [hay]!" (1547). The summoner, seeing a chance of profit, urges the devil to lay claim to what the carter has given him, but the devil declares this impossible on the basis of the theory that the speaker of these words did not intend their apparent meaning. He proves his theory by showing the summoner what happens when the cart is successfully freed from the mud. The carter, quite naturally, if irrationally, reverses his curse to a blessing because, as he says, his cart is now free and that's what he wanted. Both curse and blessing, contraries in form of speech, have exactly the same intention. As the devil says, "The carl spak oo thing [said one thing], but he thoghte another" (1568). What, then, is the summoner to make of the relation between thought and speech, not to mention the audience?

But the demon's lessons are not over. The pair next encounters a poor widow, whom the summoner attempts to frighten into paying a fine for an offense she has not committed. The summoner threatens to seize the widow's new pan when she claims to have no money, and so incensed is she by the false charges against her that the widow curses her tormenter, consigning both summoner and pan to hell.

The devil immediately asks the widow whether what she says is what she means. She modifies her speech somewhat by adding that unless he repent, she really wishes to see in hell the summoner, "And panne [pan] and al" (1629). Upon the summoner's declaration that it is not his intention to repent, the devil claims what is his, summoner and pan, and carts them off to hell.

The devil is a subtle trickster, as we see, for it is finally not because of the widow's intention that the summoner is sent to hell but, of course, by the summoner's own evil intention declared late in the tale but formed early in his brotherhood with the devil and earlier still in his vicious life. In both examples, that of the carter and that of the widow, authorial intention appears to be all powerful in determining the effect of language on reality, but as we see, it is not the carter's curse or blessing which gets him out of the mud, but rather his horses' strength. Likewise, regardless of the widow's intent, it is the summoner's viciousness that leads him to hell. The summoner and the devil act as audience to these two authors' curses, and it would seem both examples show, contrary to the devil's theory, that authorial intention only appears to determine the relationship between language and reality, whereas in the encounter with the widow, it is audience intention, represented by the summoner, that really counts.

But what about that pan? Off to hell it went, too, despite its presumed innocence and lack of all intention, by the sheer power of authorial intention. The fate of the pan, it seems, is a comic hint at the more complete solution to the dilemma in the *Friar's Tale*, the relationship between the intention in language and its effect, for it is the pan that prevents us from going uncautiously to the extreme and regarding the speaker's intention as having no effect whatsoever on his speech. But the idea that the speaker's intention can transform reality is as absurd as thinking a pan can go to hell. The devil and the summoner are two different kinds of nominalists. As the devil indicates in his explanation of the carter's language, there is no relation between language and reality and words mean whatever the speaker wants. The summoner assumes in his attack on the widow that the truth of her speech and intention, grounded in her innocence and virtue, are no barrier to the ability of language to describe and create the opposite. Since there is no truth, words mean nothing at all.

While some in the audience are perhaps shrewd enough to perceive the duplicity of the demon's theory, the Friar himself, alas, seems to go with the summoner of his tale, from the frying pan to the fire. While it has been the Friar's authorial intention to reveal the summoner of the *Canterbury Tales* as a moral degenerate, he has, because of overreliance on the power of authorial intention and a dismissal of the relationship between language and truth, condemned himself in the same terms and become the hated summoner of his own tale.

The Narrator has already introduced the Friar in the *General Prologue* through description of his corrupt activities. Chief among them is his attempt to defraud poor widows through his ability with language. His description of the summoner's attempt to extort money from a poor widow is bound to lead the audience to associate the two, as does the close similarity of vices attributed by the Narrator to the Friar himself.

The Friar as author does, however, succeed in his intention of defaming the Summoner, not simply because of his will to do so, but because of the correct correspondence of his language to the reality that the audience can see for itself in the character of the Canterbury Summoner. But his language reveals much more than merely what its author intends, exposing the author himself as morally and intellectually corrupt. The ultimate revelation of the *Friar's Tale*, however, is controlled by Chaucer, the ultimate author, and is that of the cognitive nature of language itself as originating in subjective intention but leading to objective representation of what is.

The several other pilgrims described in the *General Prologue* are figures representing similar virtues and vices in various combinations, constructed by the author in ways similar to those we have seen. A more detailed examination of a few of these figures and the tales they tell will, I hope, further uncover what the *Canterbury Tales* is ultimately about.

y insisting on the function of the Pilgrim-
rter; on the other hand, the interjection has
insisting on the fact that the *Canterbury*
ce is inevitably reminded of the book's Au-
d we are bound to recall that Chaucer the
he other pilgrims, a creation of the imagi-
y Chaucer, author, living in London, Eng-
nce, are forced to hold firmly in mind the
ive. Made self-conscious of our sphere of
stener capable of closing the book, or leav-
to another tale, we temporarily lose our
ns as real, and our role, our responsibility,
icipation in the fiction of the *Canterbury*
his being so, while the Narrator's plea for
ucer-Author's ironic veto of it, the whole
the interjection proves to be an effective
re those who can resist plunging into the
er can deliver the goods as advertised.
ve necessarily regard the pilgrims as a fic-
evertheless, that retains a degree of verisi-
that are told to it. The Canterbury level
for these stories and permits us to take a
he effect of fiction upon "reality." Such a
les a subject above and beyond the nar-
ies: that of how fiction works. Chaucer
y from tale to tale to explore this subject

ogue to his tale, the Miller institutes the

l nat been inquisityf
ee, nor of his wyf.
Goddes foyson [plenitude] there,
rest] nedeth nat enquere.

· 6 ·

Language Redeemed

The Miller's Tale

Author and Prologue. The controlling metaphor of the *Canterbury Tales* is the pilgrimage, a journey made by men and women to a religious monument, a sacred place, for the purposes of penance. Basic to the pilgrimage is recognition of one's personal disorder and the desire to reconstruct order in the self through the discovery and reaffirmation of order in the world. In a pilgrimage like Chaucer's, created by the telling of tales with a confessional character, it is essential that the pilgrims, as audience, understand clearly the stories they hear, and that the pilgrims, as authors, understand the implications of their own stories, in order to perceive how these tales have ordered or disordered the worlds they describe. It is essential, that is, if fiction has the power to redeem itself.

The *Knight's Tale* depicts a world, and the human psyches in it, as disordered and inverted through passion and misperception, in such a way that the authority of reason, the authority of nature, and the authority of the state are brought low and then reestablished in the narrative that the Knight weaves. The tale achieves the extension of private disorder-order to public disorder-order partially by having as its characters kings and queens, knights and ladies, acting out their roles in an aristocratic world. The Miller, however, is irritated by the tale. Its worldview, the formal, ideal-signifying language, and its very genre provoke him: "I wol now quite [repay] the Knyghtes tale" (3127). In an orderly world, propriety would be respected in the order of telling the tales, and we would proceed from the highest social rank, in this case, the Knight, to the next highest rank for our second author. This is just what Harry Bailly intends when he invites a churchman to speak and when he attempts to silence the Miller, saying, "Som bettre man shal telle us first another" (3130). But the Miller is drunk, and the significance of this is clarified by the Host: "Thou art a fool; thy wit is overcome" (3135).

The Miller himself, then, represents the overthrow of reason in his self-advertised drunkenness, and the quality of his authorship, as well as his authority, is conditioned in this way and several others. In the *General Prologue,* he is described in physical terms that reveal coarseness and stupidity: short-shouldered, stocky, and muscular, he uses his head best in breaking down doors. He has a wide red beard and wart on his nose with a tuft of red hairs protruding from it, and his mouth (from which will emerge his tale) is described as huge as a furnace, suggesting the medieval depictions of hell as the flaming mouth of a monster devouring souls. All these characteristics and others attributed to him would be read in the medieval science of physiognomy— the interpreting of bodily characteristics as indications of the spiritual and psychological state—as revealing a pugnacious, boisterous, lecherous character. An important detail about the Miller given in the *General Prologue* is that he plays the bagpipe. In the medieval iconographic tradition already mentioned, the bagpipe, like ungraduated bells, was a negatively charged symbol because it was incapable of producing harmonious sound but, rather, squeaked and squawked in a droning cacophony connoting irrationality. The fact that the Miller leads the entire pilgrimage toward Canterbury playing bagpipes alerts us not only to the negative character of the player but, as well, to the potential disharmony of many of those who are following this music.

The Miller, established as a "Hell mouth" who speaks "in Pilates voys" (3124), intends to deny the assertion contained in the *Knight's Tale* that mundane reality is orderly, reasonable, moral, and meaningful because it is derived from a transcendental, unchanging reality "that parfit [perfect] is and stable" (*Knight's Tale,* 3009). The Miller will attempt to prove that the purpose of poetry is anything but the expression of this ideal reality, by constructing his own poetic artifact in burlesque analogy to the Knight's ideal. He does so most effectively by retaining the analogy to the ideal and then dismantling it in a riotously comic farce in which the illusionary world of his narrative comes

· 6 ·

Language Redeemed

The Miller's Tale

Author and Prologue.   The controlling metaphor of the *Canterbury Tales* is the pilgrimage, a journey made by men and women to a religious monument, a sacred place, for the purposes of penance. Basic to the pilgrimage is recognition of one's personal disorder and the desire to reconstruct order in the self through the discovery and reaffirmation of order in the world. In a pilgrimage like Chaucer's, created by the telling of tales with a confessional character, it is essential that the pilgrims, as audience, understand clearly the stories they hear, and that the pilgrims, as authors, understand the implications of their own stories, in order to perceive how these tales have ordered or disordered the worlds they describe. It is essential, that is, if fiction has the power to redeem itself.

The *Knight's Tale* depicts a world, and the human psyches in it, as disordered and inverted through passion and misperception, in such a way that the authority of reason, the authority of nature, and the authority of the state are brought low and then reestablished in the narrative that the Knight weaves. The tale achieves the extension of private disorder-order to public disorder-order partially by having as its characters kings and queens, knights and ladies, acting out their roles in an aristocratic world. The Miller, however, is irritated by the tale. Its worldview, the formal, ideal-signifying language, and its very genre provoke him: "I wol now quite [repay] the Knyghtes tale" (3127). In an orderly world, propriety would be respected in the order of telling the tales, and we would proceed from the highest social rank, in this case, the Knight, to the next highest rank for our second author. This is just what Harry Bailly intends when he invites a churchman to speak and when he attempts to silence the Miller, saying, "Som bettre man shal telle us first another" (3130). But the Miller is drunk, and the significance of this is clarified by the Host: "Thou art a fool; thy wit is overcome" (3135).

The Miller himself, then, represents the overthrow of reason in his self-advertised drunkenness, and the quality of his authorship, as well as his authority, is conditioned in this way and several others. In the *General Prologue,* he is described in physical terms that reveal coarseness and stupidity: short-shouldered, stocky, and muscular, he uses his head best in breaking down doors. He has a wide red beard and wart on his nose with a tuft of red hairs protruding from it, and his mouth (from which will emerge his tale) is described as huge as a furnace, suggesting the medieval depictions of hell as the flaming mouth of a monster devouring souls. All these characteristics and others attributed to him would be read in the medieval science of physiognomy—the interpreting of bodily characteristics as indications of the spiritual and psychological state—as revealing a pugnacious, boisterous, lecherous character. An important detail about the Miller given in the *General Prologue* is that he plays the bagpipe. In the medieval iconographic tradition already mentioned, the bagpipe, like ungraduated bells, was a negatively charged symbol because it was incapable of producing harmonious sound but, rather, squeaked and squawked in a droning cacophony connoting irrationality. The fact that the Miller leads the entire pilgrimage toward Canterbury playing bagpipes alerts us not only to the negative character of the player but, as well, to the potential disharmony of many of those who are following this music.

The Miller, established as a "Hell mouth" who speaks "in Pilates voys" (3124), intends to deny the assertion contained in the *Knight's Tale* that mundane reality is orderly, reasonable, moral, and meaningful because it is derived from a transcendental, unchanging reality "that parfit [perfect] is and stable" (*Knight's Tale,* 3009). The Miller will attempt to prove that the purpose of poetry is anything but the expression of this ideal reality, by constructing his own poetic artifact in burlesque analogy to the Knight's ideal. He does so most effectively by retaining the analogy to the ideal and then dismantling it in a riotously comic farce in which the illusionary world of his narrative comes crashing down, dragging with it the world of ideals of the Knight, against which it is poised. The vindictive author accomplishes this largely through the pervasive use of pun, the deformation of the meaning of a word so that it signifies a meaning unrelated to its usual sense.

In addition to speaking directly to, or against, the Knight, the decision of the Miller to take as the subject of his tale a carpenter made cuckold by a clerk immediately spotlights one of the other pilgrims as a special member of the audience. The device establishes a privileged relationship between this particular author and this particular pilgrim. Chaucer does this throughout the poem, sometimes creating an alliance between author and member of the audience, sometimes an antagonism. In this case it is the latter, since the Reeve immediately bristles when he learns that a character as contentious as the Miller will tell a tale about a carpenter—the Reeve's former profession! He objects that it is a sin to slander any man and shameful to defame women, but the Miller sarcastically retorts that he who doesn't marry needn't worry about unfaithfulness. He refers unflatteringly to his own wife, and suggests that the Reeve is a bit paranoiac.

All this establishes a considerable verisimilitude: these are real people, sensitive to insult and capable of teasing irony, making personal or biographical comments about each other, and quite convinced of the effect of fiction upon reality. Why else would the Reeve and the Host attempt to censure the Miller's tale?

At this very point, when the verisimilitude of the pilgrimage level is working so well, Chaucer as Pilgrim-Narrator interjects, seemingly to reinforce the realism further (I paraphrase): "Don't blame me, if you don't like what you are about to hear! The Miller is crude and so his tale is likely to be the same. I'm just reporting the facts, what really happened. You wouldn't want me to falsify 'reality' just for the sake of decorum, would you? After all, if you don't like this sort of thing, *just turn the page* ('Turne over the leef [page] and chese another tale' [3177]), you'll find moral material enough to satisfy your needs." However, Chaucer the Author has an ulterior motive. The ironic effects of such an intervention are twofold: on the one hand, a motive of Chaucer as Author is to reinforce the verisimilitude of the frame story of the pilgrimage by insisting on the function of the Pilgrim-Narrator as an honest reporter; on the other hand, the interjection has the opposite effect, for by insisting on the fact that the *Canterbury Tales* is a book, the audience is inevitably reminded of the book's Author, Geoffrey Chaucer, and we are bound to recall that Chaucer the Pilgrim-Narrator is, like the other pilgrims, a creation of the imagination of the real Geoffrey Chaucer, author, living in London, England. Hence, we, as audience, are forced to hold firmly in mind the fictitiousness of the narrative. Made self-conscious of our sphere of audienceship, as reader or listener capable of closing the book, or leaving the room, or skipping to another tale, we temporarily lose our illusion of seeing the pilgrims as real, and our role, our responsibility, and the nature of our participation in the fiction of the *Canterbury Tales* is made quite clear. This being so, while the Narrator's plea for realism can be seen as Chaucer-Author's ironic veto of it, the whole incident revolving around the interjection proves to be an effective formal technique, for few are those who can resist plunging into the *Miller's Tale* to see if Chaucer can deliver the goods as advertised.

Under these conditions, we necessarily regard the pilgrims as a fictitious audience, but one, nevertheless, that retains a degree of verisimilitude vis-à-vis the tales that are told to it. The Canterbury level provides the realistic frame for these stories and permits us to take a step backward to observe the effect of fiction upon "reality." Such a device introduces into the tales a subject above and beyond the narratives of the individual stories: that of how fiction works. Chaucer varies the device ingeniously from tale to tale to explore this subject continually.

While still within the prologue to his tale, the Miller institutes the controlling pun:

> An housbonde shal nat been inquisityf
> Of Goddes pryvetee, nor of his wyf.
> So he may fynde Goddes foyson [plenitude] there,
> Of the remenant [rest] nedeth nat enquere.
> (3163–66)

The author (the Miller) is constructing a comic and blasphemous analogy between God's mysteries and woman's private parts (*pryvetee* = secrets, mystery, but also privacy, private parts). To paraphrase: "As long as you find [foyson] plenty there," the Miller cynically advises, "never mind what happens to the rest." His subsequent tale demonstrates, at least at the level of authorial intention, the disastrous effects of ignoring his kind of counsel. The superstitious old carpenter, John, has married a young wife whom he loves "moore than his lyf" (3222), revealing him to be at once gullible and uxorious. He is easy prey for his student boarder, Nicholas, who exploits his ignorant reverence of God's *pryvetee* and the worship of his wife's *pryvetee* in order to cuckold him.

The Tale.   The word *pryvetee* and its related forms are used some dozen times throughout the tale, signifying various meanings but always relating back comically to the controlling ambiguous sense of "divine/genital," established by the Miller's initial use in his prologue. It is used, for instance, to describe another suitor's approach to Alison, for the carpenter's delectable wife is the object of adoration not only for her husband and his boarder, but also for Absolon, the parish clerk, a figure representing complete lack of discrimination. He is described as a dandy involved in activities as diverse as barbering, surgery, notarizing, dancing, acting, and playing a wide variety of musical instruments. His eclecticism is summarized by the Miller's description of his attitude to language: "But sooth to seyn, he was somdeel squaymous / Of fartyng, and of speche daungerous" (3337–38). Squeamishness and fastidiousness (daungerous) mean essentially the same thing, and the force of this oxymoron is to suggest Absolon as a character who identifies, or rather, fails to distinguish, the quite different activities of farting and speaking. This device not only lays the foundation for his hilarious error later in the tale, but also provides a trope for the very nature of his disordered understanding of reality. Suggestive of the medieval visual grotesque made up of a figure with head and genitals inverted, Absolon can't tell the difference between the organs of speech and of farting because for him language is so much hot air

Medieval grotesque used to ornament the Ormesby Psalter. MS. Douce 366, Fol. 131. From the Bodleian Library, Oxford.

expelled this way or that to achieve whatever is wished. Similarly, he uses the church censer to "sense" the women of the parish, echoing the Miller's pun, since objects, like words, have no proper function or necessary correspondents.

The association of mouth and anus in the figure of Absolon parallels and recalls the Miller's own association of divine knowledge and carnal knowledge in his *pryvetee* pun. And thus we have an analogy of two analogies, the force of which is to suggest a world, the center of which is the human groin. Moreover, it associates the author (the Miller) with his upside-down character, Absolon, who is his spokesman. Just as the Miller's mouth, an organ normally used for the expression of reason and knowledge, is described as misused and like a hellish furnace, so Absolon's mouth is described as misused and is compared to an arse.

But the Miller's pun contains much more. God's "foyson," or plenitude, refers to the mystery of God the Creator (pancreator) who from divine abundance produces the world and all that exists without any diminishing of himself. This idea is associated through the word *pryvetee* with human creation, specifically of a sexual and reproductive kind. The comic effect of the pun resides in the second association of *pryvetee*,[27] private parts:

$$
\text{An housbonde shall nat been inquisityf}
\begin{cases}
\text{of Goddes 1} \\
\text{pryvetee} \\
\text{nor of his wyf 2}
\end{cases}
$$

By associating woman's genitals with divine plenitude, the pun renders genitals comic. The effect on the first term, "Goddes pryvetee," also comic, is slightly different, since the term is made less dignified, thus burlesque. The second term, "Wyf's pryvetee," is made more dignified, thus absurd. Both terms are momentarily expanded in meaning by association with each other, as in most puns, and the humor arises from the inappropriate elevation of the low and the equally inappropriate degradation of the high.

Under other logical and linguistic conditions, God's creation is a frequent model in the Middle Ages for human creation. The artist, for instance, is often conceived as similar to God in giving form to matter. But all similarities are based on differences, and the difference between God and the artist is that God creates from nothing as "Firste Movere," as Theseus calls him, while the artist creates from what is already created, imitating, or reproducing, forms already there from matter already existent. In the sense of reproducing, the sexual metaphor is not altogether inappropriate, since men and women reproduce from a natural plenitude their own likenesses.

The pun, however, differs from the metaphor in its introduction of similarities between ideas, similarities that are illogical and fictive and arise only from linguistic similarity. It denies the basic and critical dissimilarity between the two concepts in order to create a meaning for both uses of the word that is absurd or farcical. Beyond the comic effect of the pun, the process of paronomasia[28] demonstrates more seriously the elastic and creative power of language, and in the witty and refined pun, an intellectual delight is produced that amuses.

The Miller's entire story is constructed on puns, and we find them throughout. *Queynte* (3275, 3276, 3605) is used in both its meanings of "strange" or "artful" and its meaning of "female genitals"; the first sense derives from Latin *cognitus* (known) the second derives from Latin *cuneus* (wedge-shaped). *Sencer* and *sensynge* are also played upon (3340, 3341) to create a similar sexual joke. The church censer, derived from *censier* in Old French to become *cencer* in Middle English and, before that, from *incendere* in Latin (to set ablaze), was used to burn incense in an ancient form of praise to God. *Sensynge* is, of course, our modern word *to sense*—"to feel" or "to understand." There is, obviously, nothing refined about the Miller's puns, and they all lead directly back to his image of reality as groin. It is interesting, however, that all of his puns are related to each other by the same idea they each distort: knowledge.

The primary pun, *pryvetee*, warns against inquiry and understanding, while the Miller's use of *queynte* suggests that the rational subtlety of clerks is equivalent to physical lust. The indiscriminate "sensing" of Absolon reinforces this by associating knowledge of the divine with the sensual. The Miller's use of language and of poetry is a continuous assertion, comically couched, of the equivalence of all knowledge with carnal knowledge.

It is in this sense that the *Miller's Tale* is, indeed, a rejoinder to the *Knight's Tale*, for the force of the author's insistence on the flesh elevates limited experience, particularly sexual experience, above thought and reason. Thus he, with the carpenter, ridicules the process of deduction from universal principles or ideas and offers the audience the alternative of a reality limited to puns and pudenda, in which induction is the preferred method of investigation.

The Pilgrim-Author's predilection for *jeux de mots* is echoed in the Narrator's naive stricture just before the beginning of the tale: "And eek men shal nat maken ernest of game" (3186). The Miller takes this idea a step further, again through pun, making all language a game without consequence. It is in this way that the pun, or *jeu de mot*, becomes in the art of the Miller more than a device, but rather a philosophy and worldview in which language, speech, and fiction become their distorted, grotesque opposites—nonsense, farting, and sensual reality. Just as the Miller, beginning with an allusion to God's creation of the world, derives from it a parody of God's destruction of the world, so all else in his philosophy is turned to its contrary, the world upside down, and earnest made game.

The other major comic blasphemy of the tale is created by Nicholas who, to dupe the carpenter, convinces him that the second destruction of the world, a second flood, is coming. John's conception of reality makes this easy. Behind his superstitiousness lies a primitive idea of the correspondence of language to reality, akin to magic. When he finds Nicholas in a feigned stupor he invokes the names of all manner of saints, makes signs against elves and spirits, and bumbles around the house in ritualistic movements. Fearing Nicholas has gone mad from too much study, he pontificates: "Men sholde [should] nat knowe of Goddes pryvetee" (3454). The little knowledge that is a dangerous thing poses no risk to John, for he represents the simple inversion of the theory that signs represent realities; for him signs are the same thing as their significations, and the possession of these potent signs, usually, as John says, by "lewed" [ignorant] men, bestows the ability to harness the power of reality. This is, of course, the theory of magic.

Nicholas is, however, a learned man, and therefore knows that the power of language is quite other. He constructs reality itself, the prophesied reality of God's final destruction of the world, which follows the historic flood in which the Maker eradicated the abominations that had arisen in his creation. As the new creator, Nicholas sets the burlesque Noah about his task of constructing an absurd system of suspended tubs in which these chosen people will survive divine wrath. So exhausting are the labors of our neighborhood Noah that even the suspense of the approaching deluge cannot keep John awake. His snoring is heard by Alison and Nicholas from their respective "arks," and they climb down to the bed below to enjoy the new covenant.

The intrusion of Absolon into this "new world" is dealt with by its makers comically, but his humiliation at the bedroom window has, like all comedy, a strong didactic content. The indiscriminate parish clerk whose mental world is upside down is confronted at the carpenter's window with an image of his personal disorder:

> This Absolon gan wype his mouth ful drie.
> Derk was the nyght as pich, or as the cole,
> And at the wyndow out she putte hir hole,
> And Absolon, hym fil [to him it fell] no bet ne wers [worse],
> But with his mouth he kiste hir naked ers [arse]
> Ful savourly, er he were war [aware] of this.
> Abak he stirte [jumped], and thoughte it was amys,
> For wel he wiste [knew] a womman hath no berd [beard].
> He felte a thyng al rough and long yherd [hairy],
> And seyde, "Fy! allas! what have I do?"
> (3730–39)

Faced with how shockingly and brutally real things can be, Absolon begins to put order into life in a way reminiscent of medieval penance:

> His hoote [hot] love was coold and al yqueynt [quenched];
> For fro that tyme that he hadde kist hir ers,
> Of paramours he sette nat a kers [curse];
> For he was heeled of his maladie.
> Ful ofte paramours he gan deffie [declaim],
> And weep as dooth a child that is ybete [beaten].
> (3754–59)

This method of portraying vice as ugly or ridiculous, or both, was seen as a means of curing the vicious of their vice, and it is a basic, even somewhat primitive, form of psychology frequently used in the Middle Ages. Indeed, this is thought to be one of the functions of the comic grotesques and the hideous gargoyles employed throughout medieval art and architecture.

When he returns to the window with a hot poker, and Nicholas affords him the opportunity, Absolon is quite able to distinguish farting from speaking and can now put things in their proper place. The cleansing power of even a fictitious deluge seems to be beginning to work and with Nicholas's loud plea, "Help! water! water!" (3815), a fictive world of misorder tumbles to the floor.[29]

John's self-indulgent errors of understanding are punished by public humiliation when the neighbors are called in. Absolon and Nicholas undergo rather violent forms of correction in their quest to remake the world to suit their fantasies. Within the fictional world of the *Miller's Tale* we see that the burlesque deluge works as effectively as its model, Noah's flood, did in the historic world of Scripture, destroying a creation gone wrong and chastising its persona. The tale's author, however, seems to see no such thing, for to the Miller it is all "swyving," scalding, and farce.

As in many of the tales, the ironic treatment of the author of the *Miller's Tale* is achieved partly by the audience's perception of his limited understanding of his own creation. Again, typical of Chaucer's method, this is achieved by having the Miller unwittingly represent himself and his positions in the characters he makes the victims of the plot. It has already been pointed out how Absolon becomes the Miller's spokesman to a degree—the Miller speaks in Pontius Pilate's voice; Absolon plays Herod on the stage; and both are characterized by negative imagery of the mouth. But the Miller is also the cuckold carpenter in his campaign against intellectual understanding, for the author's philosophy of reality as farce, language as pun, is reflected in John's view of reality as devoid of logic and full of superstition.[30] Superstition, like pun, makes illogical connections, and nowhere is John revealed more clearly as the author's persona than in his declaration concerning study, where he echoes the Miller's motto:

> A man woot [knows] litel what hym [to him] shal bityde [happen].
> This man is falle, with his astromye,
> In some woodnesse [madness] or in som agonye.
> I thoghte ay wel how that it sholde be!
> Men sholde nat knowe of Goddes pryvetee.
> Ye, blessed by alwey a lewed man
> That noght but oonly his bileve kan [knows]!
> (3450–56)

Nicholas, far less like his creator in character on the descriptive level, is nevertheless, at the level of plot construction, the fullest manifestation of the Miller. As the Miller is out to goad and ridicule a Reeve, so is Nicholas. And in Nicholas's misuse of philosophy and history we see the Miller's rebuttal to the Knight's Platonic worldview. To the degree that the Miller has unwittingly included himself in his creation he has also unwittingly made himself the butt of his own joke, and fiction avenges the misuse of language by exposing the true nature of the author in his characters.

Most of the pilgrim audience laughs heartily, but, Chaucer-Narrator tells us, there were different interpretations of the tale: "Diverse folk diversely they seyde, / But for the moore part they loughe and pleyde" (*Reeve's Prologue*, 3857–58). The existence of more than one interpretation of the story within the fictional audience alerts us as audience to the spuriousness of the introductory statement of Chaucer–Narrator that "men shal nat maken ernest of game" (*Miller's Prologue*, 3186). The Reeve, we know, has been taken in by the misuse of language in the tale, and in failing to see through the pun on which the story is built, and in failing, as well, to distinguish reality from fiction, makes himself the carpenter of the tale and thus its butt. In a more complicated way the Miller does the same thing, trapping himself and his victim in the same net of artifice. The Knight, however, whom the Miller intended to rebuke, shows no sign of offense, suggesting, perhaps, that he is one of the less risible pilgrims, who knows how to make earnest of game correctly, and who is consoled to see how language reasserts its relation to reality, even in farce.

The Wife of Bath's Tale

Author and Prologue. Whatever may be the interpretation she places on the *Miller's Tale*, the Wife of Bath must have enjoyed it thoroughly. Her own prologue and tale are similar exercises in turning everything upside down, but with the Wife of Bath, Chaucer seems to be exploring similar questions under a different theme, a theme that the Wife herself identifies as experience and authority as alternative

means of understanding the truth. In his important study *Cha*
Fiction, Robert Burlin has shown the central importance of this theme
in all of Chaucer's work, but nowhere is it as explicitly addressed as
in the *Wife of Bath's Tale:* "She was preserved illiterate, allowed only
the puny weapon of her own 'experience' to contend with an armory
of masculine 'auctoritee'. No wonder, then, that the Wife uses any
strategy that comes to hand to establish and defend her identity. No
wonder, either, that she finds herself uncomfortably contrary, consis-
tently obliged to assume the very position she is opposing."[31] Philo-
sophically she is off to a bad start, however, since in the Middle Ages
this somewhat complicated concept of authority and experience as the
basis of human cognition normally regarded both elements as necessary for correct understanding. But the Wife is a dualist in all she
undertakes; she divides, differentiates, and emphasizes conflict wher-
ever possible.

Ideally, human knowledge of truth is achieved through both experience and authority, although each, and the sources of each, are different. In this tradition, all texts represent authority; all interpretation
is experience. The ultimate textual authority is Scripture, of course,
because God is its Author. The ideal of experience, it follows, is to be
found in the life of Christ, who is seen as the definitive interpreter of
Scripture, the paradigmatic exegete. It is here in the authoritative
Word of God as revealed in Scripture and in the historical life of
Christ, the *Verbum Dei,* that the junction of experience and authority
is to be found. Beyond these models lie numerous other examples of
authority and experience: truth is authority, language is experience;
meaning is authority, signification is experience; the knowable is authority, reason is experience; universals are authority, particulars are
experience. Usually authority is superior to experience, but this is not
always the case. Particularly when the authority is human—for instance, a man-made text—the right use of reason, which is experience,
may be the better guide. In any case, both ideally coincide in the Augustinian "good man skilled in teaching [*vir bonus discendi paritus*]"
whose experience guided by authority leads to correct perception and
communication of the knowable.[32]

The *Wife of Bath's Prologue* begins for the *Canterbury Tales* a debate on the question of marriage in which several other pilgrims participate. It is the woe in marriage that the Wife announces as her theme, while declaring that were there no authority on which to base her understanding of the subject, her own experience would be sufficient. On at least one level this is quite true, since she herself is the "author" of that woe experienced by her five husbands. Immediately, then, we see that the terms and concepts of authority and experience are to be used in several ways typical of Chaucerian irony. It is clear, for instance, that the Wife's use of "experience" has little to do with Thomas Aquinas's *experimentum,* the intellectual ordering and unifying of present perceptions with previous remembered perceptions.

While the Wife's entire prologue consists of memories of her past, neither her reasoning in the present about them nor her interpretation of other tales that she hears in the present pilgrimage bring order, or understanding, or meaning to her life. To cite Burlin's convenient summary of the medieval sense of experience: "This, then, is the 'experience' that underlies the Middle English definitions. It is more than the apprehension of the senses, or a collection of remembered objects; it is a unifying activity linking actual perception to what has been apprehended in the past."[33] The Wife's sense of experience is hardly a unifying activity, but rather one that separates her from everything she seeks. As opposed to integrating present with past, it leads only to a melancholy desire for what was. As the champion of experience over authority, she fails dismally, since the one thing that eludes her is real experience in the meaningful sense. To the Wife of Bath, experience is understood only in its most literal and banal senses: it means sex and power. Significantly, in her prologue, experience is something that exists only in the past and in the future, and, as the Wife makes clear, she looks forward hopefully to more sex and power as soon as possible. Experience for the Wife has become memory and anticipation without reality in the present.

Ironically, it is to authority that the Wife appeals in her assertion of the superiority of experience, and we are treated to a sustained demonstration of reason applied to text. She begins with scriptural stories

of the wedding at Cana (John 2.1) and the oft-married Samaritan encountered by Jesus at the well (John 4.6ff). Her exegesis of these pas-
sages is forthright: she has no idea, she declares, what they could
possibly mean! She is much more comfortable with the Old Testament,
particularly the commandment of Genesis, "Go, wax and multiply!"
Wax she will, but she prefers division and subtraction to multiplying
and goes on to cite the command that *husbands* must leave fathers
and mothers, dividing it from the commandment to wives about their
obligations.

Several scriptural figures are used to characterize the Wife. We recall
her introduction in the *General Prologue*: "A good WIF was ther OF
biside BATHE, / But she was somdel deef [somewhat deaf], and that
was scathe [a pity]" (*General Prologue*, 445–46). Her own reference
to the Samaritan woman whom Jesus meets by a *well* identifies her, a
woman from near *Bath*, with that other, five-time-wedded figure. But
the Samaritan understands the words of Christ ("I perceive that thou
art a prophet" [John 4.19]), whereas the Wife is "somdel deef" (446).
She prefers to be the vessel of wood or earth (dishonor) rather than
one of gold or silver (honor) (2 Tim. 2.20) and is content to be humble
barley bread as long as she does not have to be refined white bread
(143–45), especially when she recalls that it was with "barly-breed
[bread]" that "Oure Lord Jhesu refresshed many a man" (145–46).
She is associated with multiplicity and the "old," both physically and
spiritually, as she complains of advancing years and as she adopts the
literalist, "old-law" interpretation of life.

The Wife's prologue is the longest by far of all the pilgrims', and in
its biographical character seems to grow into a tale in its own right,
one that is intimately related to the story of the rapist knight she tells
later on. The Wife's life, then, becomes her text and sole authority.
Since we find no indication that the account she gives is not accurate,
the fictitiousness of that text arises, rather, from the basic fiction of
its model: that is, her life is shown to be a lie, a flawed text giving no
authoritative knowledge of the real.

The Wife has a strong effect on her audience as we see when the
Pardoner interrupts her during her prologue to compliment her for

being a "noble prechour [preacher]" on the subject of marriage. She has just finished misinterpreting Saint Paul: "The wife hath not power of her body, but the husband: and likewise also the husband hath not power of his own body, but the wife" (1 Cor. 7.4). As she disjoins the unity of authority and experience, so too, here, as in all other authorities she cites, the Wife fragments the text and cites only the part that advances her interpretation: "I have the power durynge al my lyf / Upon his propre body, and noght he" (158–59). The Pardoner, like the Wife, approves the text he hears for his own reasons, and will adopt her method of interpreting texts when his turn comes. He was about to marry, he says, but has learned the disadvantages of such a course from the Wife's description of wedded life. Throughout the *Canterbury Tales*, the Pardoner is a figure anxious to conceal and to rationalize his lack of virility; his "celibacy" is thus given a rational basis in the Wife's text. But this author encourages her audience to believe that there is more complicated matter in her tale to come and by careful attention the listener, in this case the Pardoner, may better judge the proper application of the fiction they are about to hear to the reality they live.

"Telle forth youre tale . . . / And teche us yonge men of your praktike [practice]" (186–87) urges the Pardoner, and the Wife goes on to conclude this contract with the audience in the now-familiar formula: "For myn entente is nat but for to pleye" (192). The Pardoner has good reason to welcome the Wife's fiction, for as a perceptive interpreter of tales, he has already gleaned this author's poetics as one grounded in the pleasant relativist theory that isolates fiction from reality in order to assert the one for the other.

The Tale.   Although still only at the beginning of her prologue, the Wife proclaims, "Now, sire, now wol I telle forth my tale" (193), and proceeds with an account of her married life with five spouses. In a way, this point in her prologue really is the beginning of her tale, for as we shall see, her tale proper becomes a metaphoric representation of the life she describes in the prologue, while the meaning she ascribes to her autobiography is firmly grounded in fantasy.

Alisoun boasts of her triumph over her husbands and describes the techniques by which she mastered them. The husbands fall into two categories: three were rich and old but inadequate to her erotic demands; the last two were sexually vigorous but more difficult to control. In the one kind of relationship the Wife achieves half of what she desires—power; in the other, she achieves the rest—sex; but at the end of her prologue we see that she has failed to attain the unity of the two, which she desires. Like her method of reasoning, her experience is fragmented and divided, ever at war with itself, and as she attains satisfaction in one way, she loses it in another. Her situation is not without pathos, for as a sensualist and materialist, she is doomed to a life of fleeting experiences, which never quite attain the real and which are, thus, interpretable only within the limitations of the flux of time and matter. It is this materialism that gives such prominence to memory and anticipation in her moving lament:

> But, Lord Crist! whan that it remembreth me
> Upon my yowthe, and on my jolitee,
> It tikleth me aboute myn herte roote.
> Unto this day it dooth myn herte boote [good]
> That I have had my world as in my tyme.
> But age, allas! that al wole envenyme [poison],
> Hath me biraft [robbed] my beautee and my pith [vigor].
> Lat go, farewel! the devel go therwith!
> The flour is goon, ther is namoore to telle;
> The bren [bran], as best I kan, now moste I selle;
> But yet to be right myrie wol I fonde [invent].
> (469–79)

With her last husband, Jankyn, the clerk, the Wife is seen anew in the role of audience, for her learned spouse has taken to educating her through readings from several authoritative texts, which include those of Theophrastus, Tertullian, and Saint Jerome. She is a most unwilling audience, and in her fury against these antifeminist readings she demonstrates something of the powerful relation of literature to life. The tales that Jankyn reads are of evil women throughout history and legend, and they largely preach chastity and marital affection, virtues not likely to excite the Wife's sympathies. She is particularly enraged when her husband continues to read these texts instead of coming to bed, so much so that she finally tears pages from the book, strikes him, and knocks him into the fireplace. In the ensuing battle, the Wife's persistence is sufficient to overcome Jankyn's scholarship; the book is burned, and according to one party, at least, they live for a while in a harmony based upon her mastery and his capitulation, described in terms that echo those of the ending of the tale the Wife is about to tell (813–21).

The irony of the Wife's feminism as seen in her literary creation—her tale—is that the tale not only subscribes to the antifeminist cliché that all women, in their heart of hearts, desire to be raped, but it reinforces it. We see this first at the very outset, in her lament for the disappearance of incubi[34] and spirits, who, according to the Wife, were capable in former ages of relieving women of reticence in sexual affairs, and perhaps teaching them a thing or two. In her day, alas, there were only inept (or, perhaps, incapable) begging friars lurking behind every bush. We see the pro-rape theme next in the construction of the tale, in which female authority forgives rape, and we see it finally, when the denouement of the tale becomes an occasion for the universalized mutual rape of mind as well as body. As a tale to illustrate her theme, in which female authority deposes male authority, it serves particularly poorly, just as her apologia in her prologue turns her argument upside down. For in the Wife's "faerie-lond" there are no men or women, just morally androgynous personifications of herself, and the dialectic that she attempts to set up between the male and the female shows itself false. The only authentic figures of womanhood and manhood are the aggrieved maiden seeking justice and the abdicating King Arthur possessing just authority, and these two characters are quickly disposed of by the carnal author to make room for the personifications of herself in the queen, the hag, and the knight.

The queen's usurpation of authority and the transformation of justice into a game prefigure the hag's preempting of the knight's will at the end of the tale, turning moral choice into an illusion of shape-shifting and fantasy. But this inversion has already been established for the tale in the knight's aggression against the maid, in which he has allowed the hag of lust to usurp the moral choice of his victim, imposing his will on hers. Thus the fantasy of the Wife's world is that of the shell game, and the con man, where despite the physical shape-shifting of the tale and the conceptual shape-shifting of her interpretation, nothing changes because nothing has any substance to change. Feminism is another form of antifeminism, love another form of lust, and the possibility of rational understanding, a fantasy.

In the conclusion to the *Wife of Bath's Tale* we see the triumph of her theme—tyranny. The author herself is the rapist knight. In her relationships with her five husbands, she has imposed her will and her desires; in her exegesis of Scripture and authoritative texts, she has imposed her interpretation. She abuses both. Authority, represented by the king, would have inflicted the appropriate punishment on the violent knight, but the Wife in her role as fairy queen commutes his sentence in order to rape him back in a kind of eye-for-an-eye ("gat-tooth-for-gat-tooth") justice. The knight will be raped morally when he relinquishes his integrity to the hag and gives up the power of choice in order to live happily ever after in the world of rape, which the Wife as author promotes. But, as we have seen, he has already accomplished this, without any help from the hag, in his encounter with the maiden, by abdicating to carnal impulse. He has, as it were, raped himself, just as the tale's author, the Wife of Bath, who has created him and the theme of rape, is a perpetual self-rapist.

The Wife's tale is set in the past, for which she expresses a nostalgic preference. It is a past so remote as to constitute for Chaucer's time an epoch of myth and fantasy, and it is this fantastic dimension that makes "th'olde dayes of the Kyng Arthour" so much more attractive than the present to the aging Wife. As in her personal past history there were youth, vigor, and unlimited sensuality (or so she now believes), so she posits in the days of Camelot a world of magic and lawlessness. Nowadays, she laments, a woman may go where she pleases with no fear of rape, for all the fantastic elements have been chased from the world by religion and law. In the world that the Wife constructs for her tale, all desires, no matter how contradictory, no matter how base, come true. The author's prologue has revealed an experience of life in opposition to reality and the sorrow it entails: "Allas! allas! that evere love was synne!" (614). In her tale the opposition is resolved by doing away with reality altogether. It is only in unified reality, a reality that the Wife's dualistic experience has concealed from her, that love is never sin. She therefore seeks this unification in fiction, both in the necessarily incomplete fiction of her life and in the more complete fiction of her tale.

What law is found in fairyland is soon overturned when Arthur, like the Wife's husbands, capitulates to the queen and her ladies. Feminine justice seems more merciful, since unlike established law, which prescribed death for rape, the queen merely assigns a riddle: "What thyng is it that wommen moost desiren" (905); only in failing to obtain the right answer will the knight die. The false solutions to the riddle offered to him by those he questions constitute a justification of the author's theoretical position, for they are, by and large, the same as the accusations against women that her last husband asserted: desire for wealth, flattery, lust, and license. The true answer comes by magic when in the place where he has been watching a fairy dance, he discovers a "wyf"—old and foul—who teaches the young knight, just as the Pardoner had urged the author to do, the right response. The knight thus wins his life and the old hag a young husband by the formula that what women most want is power over men. But the knight finds that he is immediately faced with still another riddle, which, like the first, is deeply rooted in dualism: how can a woman be both beautiful and faithful?

Through the fiction of her tale the author has fulfilled her desires and resolved the oppositions they engendered in life. In the allegory of her tale, the narrative relates only to the biography of her own desired future life, not to a higher level of meaning in reality external to the text. Merging with her characters, she is the raped maiden, but delighting in the lawless and violent sexuality she complains has disappeared from the contemporary world; she is the queen wresting from her husband the administration of the law; and she is, of course, the hag, suffering the rejection of the youthful knight because of her age. But in fairyland and in fiction this, too, is easily overcome: the author and the knight merge into one, in a dialogue between young husband and old wife that constitutes a monologue in which the author communicates only with herself.

The Pardoner's Tale

Author and Prologue.   There are several similarities between the Wife of Bath and the Pardoner, not the least of which is the intimate relation between the prologue and tale of each author. If it can be said that the basis of this relation between prologue and tale in the Wife's case is that she denies and destroys reality to make her fictional life valid, perhaps it may then be said that the Pardoner in turn destroys fiction in order to complete the process of rendering everything subjective and meaningless. In this sense they are in league with each other, and we see this in several ways. Whereas the Wife may be seen as a figure who distorts reality through a carnal willfulness and weakness of which she is only partially aware, the Pardoner emerges as a highly astute figure who has developed his depravity into a powerful intellectual theory, which in his prologue and tale he attempts to impose on the pilgrimage in order to destroy it. Unlike other flawed characters in the company who, despite themselves, reveal the intellectual or moral basis of their corruption (which, in many cases, they do not fully understand), the Pardoner intentionally exposes his vice in the prologue in order to raise evil to a theoretical level on which he can confront good. For if, in fact, the various authors of the pilgrimage have shown themselves as imperfect, each would seem to have also shown the origin of this imperfection to be misunderstanding or moral weakness. The great challenge to a figure like the Pardoner is to provide a theoretical basis for his fellow authors' misconstructions and for the audience's misinterpretations, and so trap them intellectually, as well as morally, in error. The Pardoner is, then, a formidable challenge not only to the authors of the Canterbury pilgrimage but also to the author of the *Canterbury Tales*, and to its audiences.

The nature of that challenge is a form of radical nominalism that calls into question the function of language in revealing truth, our ability to know truth, and consequently (in this kind of reductive logic), the objective existence of truth.

On the surface, nominalism would seem to favor the fictive use of language, since its basic claim is that universals and abstract concepts are merely names, or words, which do not correspond to or represent any objective reality. In the medieval context, however, this did not lead to a greater prestige of the imaginative use of language, but rather, just the opposite; under nominalism, the interest in language became increasingly speculative and severely logical, and literary analysis of texts lost importance.[35] The force of imaginative creation, in the medieval view, existed precisely in the correspondences that could be perceived to what lay outside the text, and part of the delight of the beautiful was generated through the multiple analogies that could be perceived between the fiction of the created artifact and the realities beyond it. Naturally, when beyond the text there is nothing other than more words, these analogies are not possible, or, at least, not delightful. In other words, the basis of fiction is reality, and when that is removed all communication becomes expository. Harry Bailly realizes this keenly, although not at a theoretical level, and continually tries to keep the "fun" in fiction; his good instinct for literature, limited though it may be, is what accounts for his eventual rage against the Pardoner.

The Pardoner is an enemy not only of orthodox medieval philosophy, but of poetry as well. His challenge to a certain theory of universals and of language is felt directly as a threat to the activity of the Canterbury authors and to the act of pilgrimage itself. By constructing the figure of the Pardoner in this way, Chaucer succeeds both in raising the theory of poetry to the level of the theme of his work, and in forcing the audience to reflect on the process of understanding and interpretation in which they are engaged.

The Pardoner's attack on the audience is launched at the outset of his introduction. The Host instructs the Pardoner to "Telle us som myrthe or japes" (319), but having perhaps perceived by his appearance and earlier behavior the Pardoner's inclination to depravity, some of the other pilgrims countermand the Host: "Nay, lat hym telle us of no ribaudye [ribaldry]!" (324). The Pardoner realizes that the pilgrims would be safer with a ribald tale than that which he has in store for them, and his ironic use of the contraries of honesty and drunkenness in agreeing to their demand expresses the disdain with which he regards their self-righteousness: " 'I graunte, ywis,' quod he, 'but I moot thynke / Upon som honest thyng while that I drynke.' " (327–28).

He begins by telling the audience how he uses rhetoric and for what purpose, revealing that in his tale-telling his theme is always the same: "*Radix malorum est Cupiditas* [Cupidity is the root of all evil]" (334) (1 Tim. 6.10). The irony that he intends is in the double sense that he preaches against the sin of cupidity while having cupidity itself as his personal motive for such preaching. For the several members of his audience who are slow in catching irony, he spells it out. With papal documents, the seals of church powers, and his own ecclesiastical title, he establishes his authority and attempts to win the respect and confidence of his audience. He then reveals his glass boxes full of old rags and bones, which the audience believes, based on the authority of the speaker, are relics. And their belief, the Pardoner tells us, is all that matters: "Relikes [relics] been they, as wenen [imagine, suppose] they echoon [each one of them]" (349). This is an important statement, for it reveals the basis of the epistemology of the Pardoner as author, and, of course, it foreshadows his final proposition to his fellow pilgrim-authors at the end of his tale.

It is unlikely that this revelation is merely more of the Pardoner's considerable cynicism toward his audience and his fellow man. Rather, it is a statement of principle. For the Pardoner, all signs are systems of discourse, language and relics alike, and what is significant in them is their manner of communication, not the validity of what they communicate. The Pardoner himself is an expert in the analysis of communications, as he amply demonstrates, and this expertise is built on the idea that no objective truth can be communicated by any system because there is none to communicate. Therefore, whatever the audience believes, or can be made to believe, through a particular discourse is, indeed, correct. That is to say, since words and other signs do not correspond to any reality other than their own process of signifying, whatever meaning they are understood to have is as good as any other; therefore, what the audience is led to believe is the best understanding that can occur. These are the pragmatics born of extreme nominalism, which make of the lie, misrepresentation, and propaganda intellectual virtues, and identify nominalism as a descendant of sophistry.

The self-revelations of his prologue present us with the paradox of the dishonest man being honest about his dishonesty. That is not to say that the Pardoner is above seduction; for, indeed, he seems to gear his words initially to the individual pilgrims seemingly most vulnerable to his rhetoric. His sheep's shoulder bone, he says, cures not only animal illnesses, but, he adds with an eye to the Wife of Bath no doubt, it cures the jealousy of husbands, even those who are quite correct in their suspicions of their wives' adultery. He has a mitten, too, that multiplies the grain it handles. The Miller is likely to have an interest in it. But his ultimate ploy is one that few in his audience are likely to be strong enough to refuse. "Anyone," he seems to say, "who is guilty of truly horrible sin, particularly women who have committed adultery, must not come forward to venerate my relics" (377–84). With this trick, as he boldly tells the pilgrims, he makes a very good living.

The Pardoner is not now playing his tricks, but describing them. Since he is a pardoner, he is more than personally concerned with sin, for penance and contrition are his professions, and he soon reveals his theory on this subject, as well. The rest of his prologue is devoted largely to the broad topic of intention and effect:

> Thus kan I preche [preach] agayn [against] that same vice
> Which that I use, and that is avarice.
> But though myself be gilty in that synne,
> Yet kan I maken oother folk to twynne [separate from],
> From avarice, and soore to repente.
> But that is nat my principal entente [intention].
> (427–32).

The Pardoner here engages a topical subject of the Middle Ages—whether an evil man can know, and thus teach, the truth. On the one hand was the position generally associated with Augustine and the Neoplatonists that true knowledge presupposed a union between knower and known, which knowledge was love. Therefore, he who did not love the truth could not be described as having real knowledge of it. On the other hand was the equally orthodox position of the Scholastics that knowledge was a function of intellect and love a function of the will. Theoretically, these faculties were separate although related, and the possibility of the coexistence of a correct intellect and a corrupt will existed. Therefore, a thoroughly evil man might know and accurately express the truth.

The Pardoner obviously allies himself with the Scholastic position, for he sees the many advantages to himself that lie therein. The fully articulated theory is sufficiently complex for there to be plenty of room for distortion. By extension, it also applies to tale-telling and thus becomes a pertinent consideration for poetry. Must a poet be a good man in order to practice his art? Or, to restate it, what is the relationship of the practice of fiction and the moral probity of the practitioner? What, in addition, is the role of authorial intention in the construction of meaning in a tale? The Pardoner provides implicit answers to these questions in his prologue and tale, and Chaucer suggests alternative responses within the larger structure of the *Canterbury Tales*.

The Pardoner ends his introductory words with a statement of principle concerning virtue, knowledge, and truth, and from this theory flows his tale. A vicious (in the original sense: full of vice) man can tell a virtuous tale, he claims, and it is clear that this implies the ability of the vicious man to know that the content of the tale is, indeed, virtuous. This is possible on the basis of the theory mentioned above that intellect and will can function independently. Thus a separation of the two faculties is introduced. This disjunction, in the Pardoner's presentation, reminds us of the Wife of Bath, who separates and divides, but never unifies, and like her, he is engaged in his storytelling in a plan to separate word from meaning, language from reality, in such a way that signs will mean anything he wants them to.

That a vicious man can tell a moral tale indicates that there really exists a moral truth that can be known. But the separation between universals and particulars is posited on the idea that if there is universal truth, it cannot be known because only particulars can be known. The further separation between signs (words, things, and concepts) and what they signify (represent, symbolize, make known) makes impossible both real knowledge of the truth and accurate expression of it. Thus, analogies between these separations can be, and in the case of the Pardoner certainly are, misleading. In Scholastic theory the truth spoken by a vicious man remains the truth, totally independent of his love or knowledge of it. Indeed, it is precisely because of its independent existence that the truth can be attained by the correct intellect despite the subject's moral condition. In nominalist theory, on the other hand, the intellect, regardless of its condition, cannot know anything beyond what the particulars of experience yield. The Pardoner, whose intellect is governed by the principle that truth cannot be known because reality is essentially a linguistic construct, can only preach the most relative kind of morality and will only create fiction of the most self-referential kind.

The Pardoner, then, because he believes that truth can never be known, lies through mental reservation in his claim about the easy accommodation of immoral author with moral fiction, just as he lies in his claim concerning the efficacy of false relics for the repenting of sin. Whereas a genuine desire to turn away from error remains genuine regardless of the authenticity of any sign which may have inspired it, the Pardoner is saying, as if in response to the Wife's earlier lament about sin and love, that "there is no sin." In this view, the repentance related to sin is illusory, and the words, objects, and ideas employed to produce this illusion are of little consequence, as long as they are believed. Reality has become an enormous pile of old rags and bones.

As with other figures of the pilgrimage, Chaucer (as author) establishes the significance of the Pardoner by his appearance and by the authoritative texts he gives him to cite. In the *General Prologue*, several details of the Pardoner's description suggest effeminacy and even eunuchry. The Narrator clearly sees and states the physical dimension of the Pardoner's condition through equine analogies: "I trowe [believe] he were a geldyng or a mare" (691). His sexual orientation is alluded to in the description of his relationship with the apparently leprous Summoner: "Ful loude he soong [sang] 'Com hider, love, to me!' " (672). The Summoner, it is said, bore him a "stif" (673) accompaniment. The Pardoner's lack of virility, his sexual impotency and sexual orientation, are not the result of genetic chance, a dominant mother, or the unfortunate consequence of disease, as our modern sciences might try to explain such characteristics. Instead, according the the medieval science of physiognomy, the Pardoner's physical endowments and health are direct reflections of his intellectual and moral condition,[36] and the same holds true for all the pilgrims. Just as his intellect is divorced from reality, self-referential, and incapable of fruitful relation with the world, so his sexuality is narcissistic, divorced from nature, sterile, and nonlife-giving. In this way Chaucer incarnates in the very physical condition of the Pardoner the philosophy and morality that the pilgrim will attempt to promote.

The Pardoner's perverse use of Scripture also harmonizes with his other characteristics. Like the Wife, the Pardoner refers only to that part of the text that serves his immediate purpose, usually distorting it, and Chaucer relies on the audience's familiarity with the true sense of the text to introduce a meaning ironically contrary to that which the Pardoner intends. Such is the case with the Pardoner's motto, "*Radix malorum est Cupiditas*," which he takes from Saint Paul's letter to Timothy (one of Paul's most prominent disciples), in which Paul gives instructions on the creation and maintenance of the Christian community. Much of the letter is concerned with false teaching and empty speech, and these are connected with cupidity by Paul: "Now the end of the commandment is charity out of a pure heart, and of a good conscience, and of faith unfeigned: From which some having swerved have turned aside unto vain jangling" (1 Tim. 1.5–6). Chaucer encourages and expects his audience to go beyond the lines of the text quoted by his pilgrim and to consider it in its wider context, which ironically reflects on the storytelling author-pilgrim.

There is much in the Pauline text from which the Pardoner extracts his dictum that reflects directly on the Pardoner himself, but perhaps nothing quite so pertinent as the following: "He is proud, knowing nothing, but doting about questions and strifes of words, whereof cometh envy, strife, railings, evil surmisings, Perverse disputings of men of corrupt minds, and destitute of the truth, supposing that gain is godliness" (1 Tim. 6.4–5). The irony of the Pardoner's citing of Saint Paul is not only that the Pauline text exposes the vice of the very one who cites it, but also that it provides an alternative position on the function of language to that held by the Pardoner. Paul's view, stated here and elsewhere, is that true language and true doctrine come directly from God so that man may know the truth, which is divine in origin and eternal: "Whereunto I am ordained a preacher, and an apostle, (I speak the truth in Christ, and lie not;) a teacher of the Gentiles in faith and verity" (1 Tim. 2.7). Thus, before the pilgrim-author has succeeded in establishing his intended meaning, the text is invested by a higher authorship with an alternative meaning capable of changing the nature of the whole text. The audience need only be capable of finding it.

The Tale. Apparently originating in the East in Buddhist literature, versions of the *Pardoner's Tale* are found throughout the world in all times up to our own (John Huston's film *The Treasure of the Sierra Madre* is such a version). Its timeless appeal certainly has something to do with its enigmatic quality and the multiple layers of meaning and of irony it contains. Chaucer's original contribution is in the development of the figure of the old man who points the way to the final denouement. Chaucer's rendering of the tale, however, is one that maintains the commentary of the Pilgrim-Author throughout in the form of the sermon, which also characterized his prologue. Having established the three protagonists of the tale as figures of capital sins, many of which he has accused himself of earlier, the author interrupts the narrative of the tale to comment on its moral significance.

Gluttony, avarice, and idolatry are the chief sins of the Pardoner's characters, and as he enumerates and describes them he also shows them to be related to each other. Appealing to a series of ancient sources, including both wise pagans and Scripture, the Pardoner creates a powerful condemnation of these sins:

> Allas! a foul thyng is it, by my feith,
> To seye this word, and fouler is the dede,
> Whan man so drynketh of the white and rede
> That of his throte he maketh his pryvee [privy / toilet],
> Thurgh thilke cursed superfluitee.
> (524–28)

In this formulation, the Pardoner alludes to the relationship between the word and that which it signifies, declaring the reality (gluttony or fornication) the signifier, to be more than the "word" (525), or signifier, but, also, the word to be appropriate to what it expresses; both are "foul." However, were the author sincere in this belief, he would personally repudiate the thing he so describes. Rather, in the case of the Pardoner, who has openly established himself as the personification of these vices, we are treated to a display of rhetorical skill, for he is engaged in creating a fiction about three characters guilty of these vices. By interspersing the fictional narrative with a discourse on the nature of those sins, he deliberately blurs the boundaries between the fictional universe of the tale and the real world to which it should correspond. In other words, by reweaving into the fiction the lesson, or meaning, that may be derived from it, the Pardoner attempts to neutralize that meaning by making it fictive.

Like the Pardoner himself, the three rioters of his tale take signs of all kinds for reality. Hearing that Death has slain one of their companions, they set out to find and to slay Death, swearing by "God's bones" to accomplish the deed before nightfall. This additional reference to bones recalls the author's earlier description of his false relics, and associates the rioters' quest to control the reality of death with the Pardoner's theory of reality as illusion. This brotherhood, whose members have sworn to live and die for each other, encounter in their quest an old man whose quest is not to slay Death but to join it, to remedy a life overextended and empty of vigor. His instructions to the youths are correct:

> To fynde Deeth, turne up this croked wey,
> For in that grove I lafte hym, by my fey,
> Under a tree, and there he wole abyde;
> Noght for youre boost he wole him no thyng hyde.
> Se ye that ook? Right there ye shal hym fynde.
> (761–65)

The old man not only pursues Death, but knows where, for all but himself, it is to be found, as his advice to the youths demonstrates. Yet he, himself, is unable to possess Death, condemned, as he tells us, forever to wander in search of what he knows but cannot become one with. Like the Pardoner, according to his own boast, the old man can lead others to what they seek, but is forever separate from it. The three rioters conceive of reality in a material and literalist way, thinking that death is a tangible, and thus controllable, phenomenon. Their dedication to food and drink is another dimension of their materialism, and so for them, signs, words, and concepts, such as the death bell they hear, the oaths they swear, and Death whom they pursue, contain no greater reality than their experiential existence. The old man, on the other hand, has lost this naive enthusiasm for the world of particulars, having long lived the bitter experience of a radically nominalist world disconnected from the real. He has become the empty sign: "Lo how I vanysshe, flessh, and blood, and skyn! / Allas! whan shul my bones been at reste?" (732–33). Still another reference to bones! He is the very sign of Death by his appearance and words, but he cannot connect with the reality that he signifies and remains a particular in search of a universal. He is the living death, the oxymoron, the contradiction that so permeates the Pardoner's prologue and tale.

All the characters of the tale, then, constitute the pilgrim-author and reveal him. The Pardoner's gluttony and swearing is echoed in the rioters who further establish his materialist-relativist philosophy in the narrative, while his eunuchry and spiritual oldness are reflected in the old man's physical lifelessness; that figure further establishes his author's nominalist philosophy in the tale through his isolation from what he knows. The tale is brought to a wonderfully ironic end through the Pardoner's brilliant use of a Eucharistic metaphor when, having found gold instead of Death under the tree, one of the trio is sent for bread and wine to celebrate their fortune. After murdering their brother, who has brought back the food, so as to divide the gold between them, the two survivors drink the wine, which the younger victim has poisoned in the hope of having the treasure all for himself. For the first and only time in the tale, the sign (gold: cupidity) and what it signifies (death) are brought together to the confounding of character and author alike.

At various levels of the tale, the Pardoner's authorial intentions are fulfilled. As a moral sermon the tale conditions the audience to repent of the various sins that they have seen so dramatically depicted and punished, and as an intellectual proposition it sufficiently confuses the nature and efficacy of signs so as to gain possible acceptance for his nominalist literary theory. But most important, from the author's point of view, the tale has set the stage for his ultimate extension of both theory and practice, the use of morality to destroy morality and the use of literature to destroy literature. The Pardoner hurries at the end of his tale toward that goal, immediately offering to his audience his false relics as means of redemption.

The Pardoner has good reason to hurry, realizing, perhaps, that within his tale, for all his careful rhetoric, lurks another possible significance antithetical to the meaning and application he intends. The longer the audience explores the text's allegorical relations to the world and to other texts, the more this meaning emerges from it. The bread and wine that bring death expand in significance as they are inevitably associated with the bread and wine that truly slay death; the oak under which the rioters find gold and death similarly unfolds into symbol when associated with the tree of life and the text "the wages of sin is death"; the numerous partial citations from Scripture and other authoritative texts reach out to their full contexts to create a larger and inevitably contradictory meaning to that intended by the author. But nothing so menaces the Pardoner's success as the figure of the old man who, as the personification of the author, reveals the Pardoner's way as living death. With the memory of the skeletal old man who points the way to death so fresh in their minds, how terrifying to the pilgrims must seem the old bones which the Pardoner now offers to them as relics.

In order to ensure the self-referentiality of the tale (so important to the success of his enterprise), the Pardoner attempts to extend its terms into the world of the Canterbury pilgrimage itself by urging his fellow travelers to accept his false relics and thereby give assent to the ideology of empty signs, meaningless experience, and positivist art:

> But, sires, o [one] word forgat I in my tale:
> I have relikes and pardoun in my male [pouch],
> As faire as any man in Engelond,
> Whiche were me yeven [given] by the popes hond.
> If any of yow wole, of devocion,
> Offren, and han myn absolucion,
> Com forth anon, and kneleth heere adoun,
> And mekely receyveth my pardoun.
> (919–26)

While we cannot know which, if any, of the pilgrims reached for coins in order to buy into the Pardoner's proposition, we see the destruction of his scheme when he appropriately singles out Harry Bailly as his main target. As Harry has, in fact, invented the idea of a tale-telling pilgrimage and acts as the official literary critic, his assent to the Pardoner's theory is most crucial. For, just as the pilgrimage itself is a physical journey toward an objective reality in time and space, that is, the shrine of Canterbury and its relics, which is a sign of a spiritual journey toward salvation, so too the tales told during the pilgrimage are an intellectual use of sign implying such a spiritual reality and the purposeful mental journey toward it. Harry's assent to the Pardoner's epistemological principles would have destroyed the meaning of both the physical and mental journeys and would have provided the Pardoner with the vengeance and the leadership he seems to desire.

The Host's ferocious rejection of the Pardoner's philosophy arises out of both his abilities and his limitations. Although he has shown himself throughout to be unable to interpret the tales beyond their level of entertainment, he nevertheless has a strong and correct instinct for what makes fiction work: Harry knows what constitutes tedium and what constitutes delight, and as far as his judgments go, they are correct. This common man's intuition about art's need for reality, for mimesis, coupled with his natural, virile heartiness, define Bailly as the Pardoner's contrary and his natural antagonist. When these opposites clash, the violence is considerable:

> "Nay, nay!" quod he, "thanne have I Cristes curs [curse]!
> Lat be," quod he, "it shal nat be, so theech [as I hope to
>   prosper]!
> Thou woldest make me kisse thyne olde breech [breeches],
> And swere it were a relyk of a seint,
> Though it were with thy fundement depeint [stained by your
>   buttocks]!
> But, by the croys [cross] which that Seint Eleyne fond,
> I woulde I hadde thy coillons [testicles] in myn hond
> In stide of relikes or of seintuarie [holy objects].
> Lat kutte [cut] hem of, I wol thee helpe hem carie;
> They shul be shryned [enshrined] in an hogges toord [turd]!"
> (946–55)

This very personal attack on the Pardoner addresses his intellectual position as well as his corporeal condition and is both appropriate and extremely telling, rendering the Pardoner speechless in defeat. The

Host has at once cruelly unmasked his adversary's physical deficiency and the sterility of his philosophy. "Your relics and your theories," Harry storms, "are as worthless as your testicles," thus knitting up and exposing all the elements of this author's motives and methods.

That the Pardoner's downfall comes through his misuse of relics is significant. By his forceful rhetoric he has succeeded in purging verbal signs of their significance, but his war on meaning is total. Like words, relics were also conceived of as signs, but as signs with a simpler and more direct relationship to what they signified. As the etymology of the word suggests, a relic was considered the "remains" of a person or object especially sanctified. Often they were parts of a saint's body or something that had touched the body and had thus taken into themselves a degree of the power of the sacred object. Like icons, relics do much more than represent what they signify; they cause the reality to be present: "The icon is not consubstantial with its prototype and yet, while employing symbolism, is not itself a symbol. It causes to emerge, not without a certain artistic rigidity, a personal presence; and it is symbolism which reveals this presence, as well as the entire cosmic context that surrounds it."[37]

Differing from the usual function of words, relics incarnate what they stand for and are a conduit for a power no longer present. Their authenticity, then, is more obviously crucial to their function, although, like the false words of the Pardoner, a false relic may inspire real faith and devotion. Relics and icons are, therefore, more powerful than words and yet far less supple. Language, even false language, does, in fact, participate in the making of meaning, whereas a false relic, like an impotent man, can engender nothing, as Harry Bailly so bluntly puts it. According to medieval theory, a false relic will under no circumstances have the effect it is supposed to have, although the subjective belief that it inspires may have merit as piety. The relic, then, depends completely for its power on the objective, independent existence of that of which it is the remains and the sign.

The Canterbury pilgrimage is one directed toward a relic, the remains of Saint Thomas à Becket. The Pardoner realizes that it is not only the stories told on the journey that must be the object of his attack, but also the goal of the journey itself, if he is to impose his view of reality upon the pilgrims. But at the same time that he voids words of their signifying power and relics of their incarnating power, he also assults a third category of sign, one preeminent and unique in medieval Christian thought, the Eucharist. The Pardoner's central allusion to this "sign of signs" comes in his insincere denunciation of gluttony: "Thise cookes, how they stampe, and streyne, and grynde, / And turnen substaunce into accident" (538–39).

The theory of the Eucharist is that through the repetition of Christ's words at the Last Supper, bread and wine become the Body and Blood of Christ while retaining their natural form and appearance. Through this transubstantiation the *accidents*, or visible and tangible aspects of the bread and wine, remain while the *substance*, or essence, is changed to that of the Divinity. Just as the Pardoner uses the image of bread and wine at the end of the tale to denote death, so here he uses the theory of transubstantiation to describe gluttony and luxury, and for good reason. For in the Eucharist is discovered the highest order of the real, in that it is both sign and signified simultaneously. For it is not a true sign of something else, nor only a representation, nor even an icon that calls forth the divine presence in the Eucharist, but it is a complete union of symbol and reality, which, as it is eaten by the faithful, denotes the complete union of knower and known, creator and created, universal and particular.

For the radical nominalist, the possibility that every day, in every church, the particulars of bread and wine not only communicated a universal, but became the universal of universals (Plato's *nous*, Christianity's superessential Being), posed a serious problem, and in Chaucer's time more than in any other the question of transubstantiation was hotly argued. Robert E. Nichols, Jr., in his study of the Eucharistic symbolism in the *Pardoner's Tale*, describes one side of the controversy: "Wyclif, who declared that hypocritical clergy by their actions 'ben made wafreris,' protested the fiction that any priest can 'make' the body of Christ daily by saying mass, arguing that he simply 'makes' in the host a sign of the Lord."[38]

We see how far-reaching is the Pardoner's attack on cognition when we realize that the three cornerstones of knowledge—language, icon, and Eucharist—which he attempts to undermine, constitute the epistemological structure of the Middle Ages. Just as he empties signs of their signification through his manipulation of language, and just as he demotes the function of the relic to that of the empty sign, so, too, he attempts to devalue the mystery of the Eucharist to the status of a human sign. Attempting to project his own spiritual decay onto the world through the use of fiction in his tale, this author threatens the basis of fiction itself. But in Chaucerian poetics there is within language, and thus within fiction, the power to reassert the essential connection with reality, as is revealed in this case through the unlikely agency of the Host, "moost envoluped in synne."

The Nun's Priest's Tale

It would be wrong to give the impression that Chaucer presents only one side of the question in the *Canterbury Tales* or that he constantly ironically distances himself from all his characters through wry portraiture. There is nothing in the description of the Nun's Priest, for instance, to alert us to corrupt authorship. Indeed, he is not described at all in the *General Prologue*, and his tale therefore seems more detached from the character of its author than do most others. This is appropriate since the *Nun's Priest's Tale* functions partly to right some of the wrong done to fiction in previous tales. Its most obvious response is to the *Monk's Tale*, which precedes it and which has depressed the company by its theme and bored them thoroughly by its technique. In obedience to the host's command, Sir John, the priest, promises to be merry and tell a merry tale.

The tale of Chauntecleer and Pertelote is an allegory derived from the animal fable of ancient pedigree and told in a mock-epic style, intended to burlesque the Monk's ponderous tragedies. While the tale is allegorical, what it is an allegory of is rather more difficult to unravel. It has been seen as a historical, political allegory on the reigns of King Richard II and Henry IV; as an allegorical religious satire involving various categories of clergy; and, as well, as a representation of the fall of Adam.[39] It is clear, then, simply from the number of interpretations it has inspired that the *Nun's Priest's Tale* is a rich source of meanings. Is its meaning to be found in one of these allegorical routes, in none of them, or, like Dante's *Divine Comedy*, is it a multilayered allegory that can be read with consistency on several levels at once?

Allegories are always about something, the narrative story corresponding, sometimes in a simple way, sometimes through complex relations, to another idea or narrative. There seems to be something mischievous in the way in which this "sweete preest" conceals the ultimate meaning of his tale in a too rich medley of possible meanings. What is this author's intention?

On the one hand, as has been said, the *Nun's Priest's Tale* intends to respond satirically to the bombastic style of the Monk's tale, as well as to satirize its tragic themes. It has also been seen to allude in several ways to the *Wife of Bath's Tale* and to that author's answer to the riddle of what "women most desire," as well as to her view on the relation of men and women. In a more general and sly way, the *Nun's Priest's Tale* may also address the Pardoner's view of both fiction and reality and possibly the views of several other pilgrim-authors. To the degree that it responds to several tales and interweaves their points of view into its own structure, the *Nun's Priest's Tale* is not so much an allegory of a political event or a symbolic presentation of an idea as it is a tale about how tales should work. This is not to say that the story of Chauntecleer and Pertelote is without content or meaning, or even that the meaning is totally self-reflexive, but rather that unlike the tales that have principally a philosophical point as their content, or those that have only "game" as their object, the *Nun's Priest's Tale* gathers up aspects of these different tales, demonstrates the process of good fiction, and even prepares for Chaucer's *Retraction* at the end of the work.

The *Parson's Tale* functions in a somewhat similar way. As a sermon it preaches against a number of vices and exhorts us to certain virtues, all of which have been seen before in the moral disposition of the Canterbury pilgrims and in their tales. But the *Parson's Tale* has no claim to entertainment; it is a sermon and a boring one. Indeed, the Parson says that he has no skill in tale-telling and, furthermore, doesn't desire any since he is suspicious of it. So, although the *Parson's Tale* reflects on all the other Canterbury tales, it reflects on their moral content and ignores their success or failure as good fiction.

The *Nun's Priest's Tale* seems to have no particular moral, or, perhaps more accurately, it has so many unsustained morals as to have a vague moral effect. It would seem that, instead, the way the *Nun's Priest's Tale* reflects back on the *Canterbury Tales* as a whole is in terms of the theory of fiction itself. And this reflection is deeper than just a consideration of the mechanics of good storytelling, for it says something more directly than elsewhere about the issue so frequently encountered in the *Canterbury Tales*—the function of poetic language in expressing truth.

In this way, the last pieces of the *Canterbury Tales* have something in common and may even be seen to go together. The *Nun's Priest's Tale,* in its highly rhetorical way, shows us how crucial is the way language is used in the process of revealing meaning, by showing both the danger of its abuse in fiction and its inherent ability to correct that abuse. The *Parson's Tale* provides a partial answer to the dilemma created in the *Canterbury Tales* about the function of language, by clarifying and reaffirming the orthodox truths that through language can be applied to life. Finally, in Chaucer's *Retraction* at the end of the *Canterbury Tales*, it would seem these two partial views, right content and right language, are brought together to suggest the author's view of the possibilities and limits of man's use of language to gain truth. Will and understanding, says Chaucer, are two powers that determine our ability to perceive the real. The *Parson's Tale* tells us much about will, both the corrupt will and the righteous will, which determine the intention of every story and every human expression.[40] The *Nun's Priest's Tale* is more concerned with understanding, particularly the understanding of how the intention, good or bad, gets expressed and understood.

The peculiar use the Priest makes of the animal fable immediately puts the audience off guard. Normally in such allegory, supposedly

natural characteristics of the animals involved are associated with human vices and virtues—the slyness of the fox, the courage of the lion—
to dramatize aspects of human reality. The Nun's Priest in his version
seems to have reversed the process by ascribing human characteristics—intellectual speculation, historical knowledge—to his barnyard
fowls, as if his interest were principally the philosophical and existential issues of chickendom! The task of the audience in discovering the
relation of the Nun's Priest's fiction to its reality will be a particularly
difficult one.

Chauntecleer, an inhabitant of a poor widow's barnyard, is in every
way a contrast to his human owner. The poor widow and her daugh-
ters, who make but brief appearances, are a standard medieval allegory of the Church, temporally widowed by the death of her spouse,
Jesus, and left to care for the souls of his estate. The widow is por-
trayed, as convention demands, as moderate and even frugal in her
life and diet. Beyond this description, the Nun's Priest wastes little time
developing the "allegory of the Church."

In contrast, however, to this dairy woman who owns him, Chauntecleer is kingly, decked in brilliant and royal colors, possessed of a
harem of seven hens, and, despite a bad night's sleep, aristocratic in
his bearing and diligent in his virile duties:

> He fethered [caressed] Pertelote twenty tyme,
> And trad [mounted] hire eke as ofte, er it was pryme.
> He looketh as it were a grym leoun [lion],
> And on his toos he rometh up and doun;
> Hym deigned nat to sette his foot to grounde.
> He chukketh [clucked] whan he hath a corn yfounde,
> And to hym rennen thanne his wyves alle.
> Thus roial, as a prince is in his halle,
> Leve I this Chauntecleer.
> (3177–85)

Chauntecleer's favorite mate is a courtly hen of some intellectual
substance. Pertelote possesses both beauty and brains and has, not
surprisingly, therefore, a great influence over her husband. At issue

between them is the efficacy of a dream that Chauntecleer has had, which, he believes, has warned him of danger in the real world. In the dream, the cock has seen something that in life he has never experienced before. As "I romed up and doun," he says:

> Withinne our yeerd, wheer as I saugh a beest
> Was lyk an hound, and wolde han maad areest [seized]
> Upon my body, and wolde han had me deed.
> His colour was bitwixe yelow and reed,
> And tipped was his tayl and bothe his eeris [ears]
> With blak, unlyk the remenant [rest] of his heeris [hair];
> His snowte smal, with glowynge eyen tweye [two].
> Yet of his look for feere almoost I deye [die].
> (2899–2906)

His more empirical wife will have none of this and condemns outright the medieval theory that dreams may reveal reality:

> "Avoy!" quod she, "fy oɳ yow, hertelees!
> Allas!" quod she, "for, by that God above,
> Now han ye lost myn herte and al my love.
> I kan nat love a coward, by my feith!
> For certes, what so any womman seith,
> We alle desiren, if it myghte bee,
> To han housbondes hardy, wise, and free,
> And secree [discreet], and no nygard, ne [nor] no fool,
> Ne hym that is agast of every tool,
> Ne noon avauntour, by that God above!
> How dorste ye seyn, for shame, unto youre love
> That any thyng myghte make you aferd [afraid]?
> Have ye no mannes herte, and han a berd [beard]?
> Allas! and konne ye been agast [afraid] of swevenys [dreams]?
> (2908–21)

Chauntecleer, of course, has no beard, or does he? Is he chicken or man? The rapid switch from metaphor to anatomical description, from allegory to narrative, could well confuse (and amuse) the audience. But Pertelote's use of metaphor is accidental. She is a pragmatist and empiricist, and although not above defending her theories with authoritative texts (she cites Cato), like the Wife of Bath she sides with experience and experiment. A good laxative is what Chauntecleer needs!

The audience will not have missed Pertelote's other allusion to the Wife of Bath as she contradicts directly the Wife's theory, stating rather that what women most want is a bold and dominant husband. This in no way prevents her from mastering her mate in exactly the way the Wife has done, and it is her physical charm more than her scholarship that finally persuades the uxorious Chauntecleer to ignore the relation of his dream to his life. As a critique of the Wife's philosophy and fiction, the economically established contradictions of the pretentious hen are devastating.

Chauntecleer's dream has at least two important functions in the tale, superseding its role in the plot. In one way, it creates through its relation to the other events in Chauntecleer's life—when the dream comes true—an analogy with the connection of fiction to reality, a connection that has been confused or deformed in several other tales. In other ways, closely related to this, it suggests something basic about knowledge itself, which, in fact, makes possible the relation between dream and life, fiction and reality.

Chauntecleer is described appropriately as possessing natural knowledge, called instinct among animals, by which he knows precisely the time of day: "By nature he knew ech ascencioun [ascending degree] / Of the equynoxial [equinoxial circle] in thilke toun [town]" (2855–56). In addition, through natural knowledge he recognizes in his dream the form and appearance of his natural enemy, the fox, which in life he has never seen or experienced. By this natural knowledge Chauntecleer has an ability to interpret correctly the symbols of the "text" of his dream, and he should thus be able to use his knowledge in his life and avoid disaster. As we see, Chauntecleer is not able to accomplish this last step. His knowledge is true. The beast he sees in the dream and later in the yard is a danger. His use of this knowledge is, however, faulty.

Similarly, the poetic text presenting what has never before been seen or heard, fantastic conceptions like talking chickens and foxes, may, with the proper writing by an author and the proper interpretation of the audience, illuminate something essential about the way the world really is. But the ability to interpret and to apply is crucial. The *Nun's Priest's Tale* tells us a great deal, not only about interpreting, but also about what every interpreter must know, how poetry works.

Chauntecleer, as we know, fails as audience to his own dream by not taking it seriously enough. Pertelote, who has become not only his apothecary but his literary critic, persuades him that there is no connection between text and reality and that it is all a matter of indigestion. Like the Wife, she places her faith in the senses and proposes, reminiscent of Eve in the Garden of Eden, to teach her husband all about what is good to eat:

> I shal myself to herbes techen yow
> That shul been for youre hele [health] and for youre prow
>   [profit];
> And in oure yeerd tho herbes shal I fynde
> The whiche han of hire propretee by kynde
> To purge yow bynethe [beneath] and eek [also] above.
> (2949–53)

The connection with Eve, and thus with the Garden of Eden theme, is made in the *Nun's Priest's Tale* in such a way that it bounces back and forth like a spotlight, momentarily showing Pertelote as comic temptress, illuminating the Wife of Bath as an aged Eve and the world's calamity, then flashing back on Chauntecleer, an Adam with no apple, just the worm. Like so many of the allusions in the *Nun's Priest's Tale*, the presence of the original sin theme does not provide the "meaning" of the tale, nor does its discovery reveal the *Nun's Priest's Tale* as an allegory of the Fall, but rather calls our attention to how poetry engenders meaning by the use of language. The Pertelote–Wife of Bath analogy connects to the Pertelote-Eve analogy and instantly reinterprets the *Wife of Bath's Tale* as a story told by an Eve figure. And the associations continue: just as the Wife opposed her husband's reading of books—texts that lead to knowledge–so Pertelote opposes Chauntecleer's text, the prophetic dream.

In order for a dream to contain true information about reality, albeit symbolically communicated, reality itself must be constituted by certain laws and principles that are constant and knowable. In Chauntecleer's dream, his recognition of the fox depends on there being not just innumerable individual foxes in England, but a universal "foxness" which by certain characteristics and signs is recognizable, even if not nameable, as constituting a fox. It is of some importance that when describing his dream, Chauntecleer is not able to name the beast that he has seen, but he knows it anyway. The medieval theory of dreams depended directly on a Platonic theory of the real and did not fare well among the nominalists, with their insistence on experience as the origin of knowledge and ideas. Chauntecleer knows without experience, and we see that his knowledge is true, but Pertelote cannot believe this possible since, in the perspective she embodies, only experience can bring knowing.

Pertelote, in rejecting Chauntecleer's dream, is, however, full of names, names especially of herbs, which she urges are much more real than dreams: lawriol, centaure, fumetere, ellebor, katapuce, gaitrys beryis, herbe yve; all able to be eaten up, experienced, and learned from. All laxatives for a too credulous husband. It is perhaps not without significance that several of these "names" are those of natural poisons, which had Chauntecleer eaten them all at once might indeed have permanently cured him of his credulity.[41]

Our Chauntecleer however, possesses not only natural knowledge, but intellectual knowledge as well. However, just as his natural knowledge is corrupted by his own vanity and concupiscence, so his intellectual knowledge is flawed by the same confusion over appetite and reason. Since the cock is male and male traditionally represents reason, he feels the need to teach Pertelote, female and representing appetite, all about texts and knowledge, and even condescends to translate from Latin for her: "*In principio, / Mulier est hominis con-fusio,— / Madame*, the sentence [meaning] of this Latyn is, / 'Wom-man is mannes joye and al his blis' " (3163–66).

Here again the Nun's Priest has turned the tables on literary con-vention, for the reasonable male turns out not only to be unreasona-ble, but quite ignorant. His Latin phrase means "From the beginning, woman is man's ruin." His translation of it into its diametrically op-posite meaning shows simultaneously the fragility of authority and intellect and the dependency of understanding on will. The more gen-erally understood meaning of the phrase was that the fall of "man-kind," not males, was caused through an effeminate will, and, indeed, Adam's own personal weakness, although abetted by Eve, caused the Fall. Certainly in the case of our New Adam, Chauntecleer, it is not Pertelote's argument, which he has to his own satisfaction demolished, that leads him into the fox's jaws, but rather his own sensuality and foolhardiness.

The *Nun's Priest's Tale* has been read, like Chauntecleer's Latin phrase, in any and all ways. Some have found in it the intention of the author to declare the impossibility of any firm moral position, of any valid intellectual view, and even of any poetic criteria.[42] This would put the priest firmly in the camp of the Pardoner, and make of them a pair of admirers for the Wife of Bath. Many others have taken the opposite view that the tale is a conventional allegory of one thing or another, the meaning of which is immediately transparent upon find-ing the key to the allegory. The problem may lie in the very thinness of the story itself—the cock caught by the fox—and the quite heavy rhetorical style that such a story is made to bear by the author. This combination of high rhetoric and low subject, while it clearly makes fun of the *Monk's Tale,* which precedes it, more importantly calls the attention of the audience to the way the tale is written rather than to what it says. In this way, the Nun's Priest, of all the storytellers on the pilgrimage, is most like Chaucer himself, regularly calling attention to his craft, breaking the spell of the story, winking at his audience—in short, forcing us to see how fiction works. But this is not to say that the *Nun's Priest's Tale* has no content or that it is meant to ridicule meaning. The crux of the story is Chauntecleer's fall and his escape, and in the description of those events, both the meaning of the plot and the meaning of meaning join.

Weary of intellectual debate, Chauntecleer turns to the more pleasant aspects of life, the satisfaction of the senses: his woman and his food. As he says:

> For whan I feele a-nyght your softe syde,
> Al be it that I may nat on yow ryde,
> For that oure perche is maad so narwe [narrow], allas!
> I am so ful of joye and of solas,
> That I diffye [renounce] bothe sweven [type of dream] and
>   dreem.
> (3167–71)

Many have seen in this natural lust the origin of the hero's fall, but the Nun's Priest has extended the description of the encounter between fox and cock to include something more decisive. Chauntecleer's rejection of his dream in favor of Pertelote's charms comes only after he has used his natural knowledge to satisfy his intellectual vanity in absurd intellectual discourse with the hen. That form of self-indulgence fulfilled, he proceeds to satisfy his physical vanity as well, mounting his mate some twenty times in short order. The third form of vanity that Chauntecleer exhibits is artistic vanity or pride, seen in his singing, as the fox calls it, against all the urgings of nature. Although all the forms of vanity are really one, the fox shrewdly appeals to his artistic vanity to ensnare him.

There is in the scene of Chauntecleer's meeting with the fox a certain insistence again on Chauntecleer's possession of a natural knowledge of signs and a true correspondence between those signs and truth. The scene begins with Chauntecleer's crowing at the appropriate hour, which he knows "by kynde [nature], and by noon oother loore [learning]" (3196). His sighting of the fox, which he has never experienced before, produces instinctual fear: "For natureelly [by nature] a beest desireth flee / Fro his contrarie, if he may it see, / Though he never erst [before] hadde seyn it with his ye [eye]" (3279–81). Why then, does Chauntecleer, equipped with all the knowledge he needs to survive, not save himself? Language used to misrepresent reality is sufficiently powerful to the ear of a vain audience to supplant the relationship created by nature between sign and signified and to replace it with one created by the speaker for his purposes.

The fox's flattery takes the form of a story that is likely true on the historical level, the story of Chauntecleer's father's singing and his encounter with the same fox, but on another level, quiet clear to us as audience, it reveals that Chauntecleer's sire has earlier been a victim of the fox. Chauntecleer is deaf to the deeper truth of the tale, however, because he is utterly charmed by the flattering language in which it is couched. Neither natural knowledge nor cogitation can prevent Chauntecleer from singing when he should not, and, although his initial instinct on seeing the fox was silence ("Nothyng ne liste hym [he had no desire] thanne for to crowe" [3276]), his enemy's false representation of his own natural history is sweeter than reality itself. Like so many of the pilgrims who are listening to the *Nun's Priest's Tale,* Chauntecleer combines the roles of audience and author in a flawed way. He misunderstands the fox's text because of his own vanity, and that same vanity leads him to create his own crackling text devoid of both understanding and humility.

The Nun's Priest interrupts here with a digression on flattery, which, not unlike the pun and equivocation, is a misuse of language to distort reality. Mortimer J. Donovan considers the flattery theme central to Chauntecleer's fall: "The apothegm which ends the sermon, 'Lo, swich it is for to be recchelees / And necligent, and truste on flaterye' serves to reaffirm the deeper meaning of *flaterye*—a diabolical misuse of human speech which can lead one to hell if he is slow to meet the tempter with a curse as strong as Chauntecleer's."[43]

Unlike the poisoned youths of the *Pardoner's Tale* or the perpetually enslaved knight created by the Wife, Chauntecleer is not led into final peril by his creator. The Nun's Priest's intention is not to beguile by fiction but rather to show how bad fiction can beguile. The continuous references in the *Nun's Priest's Tale,* direct and indirect, to other tales authored by other pilgrims provides a critique of how those tales worked. In the *Pardoner's Tale* the audience was treated to a superbly wrought story in which every detail of the plot contributes to the ironic ending. The equivocal meaning of the *Pardoner's Tale* is deeply hidden in its artistry. Similarly, the Wife of Bath fascinates and befuddles her audience with a delightful mixture of biography and fantasy, which largely succeeds in gaining acceptance for her flawed solution to her own riddles. Not so the *Nun's Priest's Tale*. Easy interpretations and fictive formulas are repeatedly denied by constant calling attention to the fiction itself. Saul Brody cogently remarks this essential quality of the tale: "His tale is thus paradoxically both absurd and serious, realistic and unrealistic, fictive and true, and that paradox, that tension between the literature-like and the life-like, is central to the tale. It is the source at once of much of its humor and much of its point, for through it the Nun's Priest asserts the ultimate seriousness not simply of his fiction, but of all fiction."[44]

This seriousness of fiction requires not only Chauntecleer's downfall through words misused and misunderstood, but also his rescue through the proper use of words. The hero is redeemed by language when he learns to reconstruct its proper and natural relation to reality. Having lost his innocent possession of natural knowledge through a vain and comic intellectualism, a knowing through words, Chauntecleer discovers from his terrible experience how to use words to reclaim the control of reality he originally possessed through nature. Redeeming language, he saves himself. Chauntecleer uses the same ruse to free himself that the fox used to trap him, illustrating, as the whole tale does, that language itself is capable of opposite effects and depends upon the good will and understanding of the speaker. In their final exchange, both cock and fox reveal that they have learned much about cognition and language, the one referring to seeing and blindness, the other to speaking and silence. Chauntecleer states that in the future he will know when to "wynke" and when not, and the audience of the *Canterbury Tales*, so used now to winking authors, may perhaps conclude with Chauntecleer that the time for winking is over and that, with an understanding of the seriousness of fiction demonstrated in the comedy of the *Nun's Priest's Tale,* they have learned both au-dienceship and authorship. Just as Chauntecleer's ability to compre-hend the texts he encounters is essential to his survival, so the pilgrims' ability to interpret the texts they hear is crucial to their ability to tell their own tales.

Having called a halt to artistic and intellectual winking through his redeemed hero, the Nun's Priest concludes his words with Saint Paul's dictum "al that writen is / To oure doctrine [learning] it is ywrite, ywis" (3441–42).

· 7 ·

Conclusion

The contract between author and audience in the *Canterbury Tales* is a complicated one, which we have earlier summarized with the lines from *Troilus and Criseyde* indicating its basis as "good intention" on both sides. Authorial intention in the *Canterbury Tales* is discovered only through a process of interpretation and understanding of the text, which reveals at the same time the nature of the good intention of the audience, as well. At that point, we see that the motive and under-standing—the two meanings of *entencioun*—are the same for both, and that audience and author merge.

In his exploration of the nature of the relationship between author and audience, Walter J. Ong describes Chaucer's grappling with the literary problem that faced him in the writing of the *Canterbury Tales*: "He sets the stories in what, from a literary-structural point of view, is styled a frame. A group of pilgrims going to Canterbury tell stories to one another: the pilgrimage frames the individual narratives. In terms of signals to his readers, we could put it another way: Chaucer simply tells his readers how they are to fictionalize themselves."[45]

In Chaucer's case, however, this is a special process, for it involves, in addition to fictionalizing the audience, fictionalizing himself as au-thor, as well, as we see in the character of the Narrator, and fiction-alizing the very concept of authorship and audienceship. But as with other Chaucerian uses of fiction, audience and author are rendered fictive as a means to their being finally returned to reality better able to know it because of the process. Just as he does not restrict the au-dience to a one-sided contract, so Chaucer does not allow the audience to remain fictional. Audience and author merge at certain levels of the text.

At a level within the text itself, we see the Canterbury pilgrims reg-ularly transform themselves from audience to author and back again as each tells his or her tale. Yet, whether as author or as audience, each pilgrim is always a creature of the author beyond the text, as we are allowed to see through a variety of poetic devices. In Chaucer's aesthetic, this functions as a paradigm for all the relationships of audience to artifice, in which, through a process that is essentially allegorical, the restricted roles of author, audience, fiction, reality, speaker, and listener are transcended and are integrated, so as to form a didactic model of man's relationship to his Creator, as well as to other creature-authors.

At another level, close to the text but outside it, the reader is more intimately associated with the historical Chaucer the Author. The functions of the Narrator and of the realistic frame of the *Canterbury Tales* are fundamental to the construction of this level, for while we, as readers, are often within the text listening, like any of the pilgrims, to various tales, we are frequently and deliberately expelled from this fiction to a level where we meet the real author and share with him his customarily wry view of the Narrator, of the Host, and of the other pilgrims. This distancing of Author from Narrator is, perhaps, most clearly seen when Chaucer-Narrator is invited by Bailly to tell a tale, like the other pilgrims, and fails miserably in the art of which the historical Chaucer is a world master. Here we see not only a prime example of author turned audience and of creator turned creature (for the Narrator is on one level author-creator of the the *Canterbury Tales* and, as reporter, its audience), but we observe, as well, how Chaucer gets us from one level of the text to another. With the failure of the Narrator as poet we have only one recourse for guidance, and that is to Chaucer the Author, who is found outside the fiction at the trans-textual level. Through our increasing intimacy with Chaucer the Author, which seems at times almost conspiratorial, a still further level of audienceship is established.

The realism of the frame, reinforced by the didactic content of the tales, which the reader is encouraged to apply personally, makes us sometime pilgrims, as it were, on this fictional journey to Canterbury. We listen, just as the other pilgrims do, to the tales told along the way. But the other travelers get to tell tales as well as hear them and have a go at being authors, just like Chaucer. What about us? Chaucer reminds us frequently in one way or another that, like him, we are not really on the road to Canterbury but listening to a poem or sitting alone somewhere, reading the text. This increases our intimacy with him, because Chaucer, too, sat alone somewhere and wrote the text, and he later stood somewhere and read it aloud. But our association with Chaucer does not destroy our relation to the Narrator and the other pilgrims; it only distances it and transposes our experience to another arena, the same one in which the historical Chaucer has created his poem—the real world.

In the *Retraction* at the end of the *Canterbury Tales*, Chaucer raises the subject of his real life and literary work, apologizing for any failures in them and attributing their successes to "Jhesu Crist, of whom procedeth al wit and all goodnesse" (1081). Chaucer's perspective here—still within the poem—has switched from creator of fiction to creature of God. Any of the creatures of the *Canterbury Tales* might have said likewise, and some do, recognizing their creaturely dependence on their "auctor." Given Chaucer's formula for fiction, in which characters become authors, authors become audiences, and creatures become creators, we, as readers, discover through our association with Chaucer on this third level of audienceship that the existential formula is the reverse of the fictional: we, as audience, must become authors, and our stories will be, like those of the Canterbury pilgrims, as good as our lives. As authors we become simultaneously characters in a larger "frame," that of human history, governed by the "authorial intention" of its Creator, which our individual stories either hinder or advance; in our role as creators we, too, like the pilgrims and like Chaucer, are governed by our simultaneous status as creatures. The direction of all these analogies between levels points outside the poetic text to the "text" of created nature, and beyond that text, and beyond all discourse, to the final source of all texts and all discourse in the uncreated Author.

From this perspective, Chaucer's theoretical interest in poetics and imagination can be seen to have developed into an important philosophical and moral perception into the nature of the real and the role of art in illuminating the real. Far from being merely conventional, Chaucer's own last words on the subject, quoting from 2 Timothy 3.16, can be seen as the mature theoretical basis of his art: " 'Al that is writen is writen for oure doctrine,' " and, says Geoffrey Chaucer, with finality, "that is myn entente" (*Retraction*, 1083).

Notes

1. Very little is known of Geoffrey Chaucer, but many years of detective work have uncovered enough facts to develop a likely biography. The introduction to any of the larger editions of Chaucer's works will give a good summary of what is known and surmised about his life.

2. See Robert O. Payne, "Chaucer and the Art of Rhetoric," in *Companion to Chaucer Studies*, ed. Beryl Rowland (New York: Oxford University Press, 1979), 42–64.

3. For a summary of the classical intellectual background, see Winthrop Wetherbee, "Some Intellectual Themes in Chaucer's Poetry," in *Geoffrey Chaucer: A Collection of Original Articles*, ed. George D. Economou (New York: McGraw-Hill, 1975), 75–91.

4. Herbert Read, *Icon and Idea: The Function of Art in the Development of Human Consciousness* (New York: Schocken Books, 1965), 29.

5. For a good analysis of the events of the period, see John A. F. Thomson, *The Transformation of Medieval England: 1370–1529* (London: Longman, 1983); M. H. Keen, *England in the Later Middle Ages* (London: Methuen and Co., 1973).

6. Dante Alighieri, *Dantis Alegherii Epistolae: The Letters of Dante*, 2d ed., trans. Paget Jackson Toynbee (Oxford: Clarendon Press, 1966), Letter 10.7, 199.

7. For an exhaustive discussion of this subject, see Caroline Spurgeon, *Five Hundred Years of Chaucer Criticism and Allusion (1357–1900)*, 3 vols. (Cambridge: Cambridge University Press, 1925). Short selections of criticism, including modern samplings (to 1968), occur in J. A. Burrow, ed., *Geoffrey Chaucer: A Critical Anthology* (Harmondsworth: Penguin Books, 1969). Quotations in this chapter from Sir Philip Sydney, John Dryden, William Blake, and Samuel Taylor Coleridge can be found in this book.

8. Ezra Pound, *ABC of Reading* (New York: New Directions Paperbook, 1960), 99.

9. T. S. Eliot, *Selected Poems* (London: Faber and Faber, 1954), 51.

10. See George Lyman Kittredge, *Chaucer and His Poetry* (1915; reprint, Cambridge, Mass.: Harvard University Press, 1960).

11. The most important of these is Ralph Baldwin, *The Unity of the Canterbury Tales* (1955); reprint, New York: AMS Press, 1972).

12. D. W. Robertson, Jr., *A Preface to Chaucer: Studies in Medieval Perspective* (Princeton: Princeton University Press, 1962).

13. Philotheus Boehner, in the introduction to *Ockham: Philosophical Writings*, ed. Philotheus Boehner (Edinburgh: Nelson, 1957), ix.

14. For a lucid discussion of the long history of the "problem of the universals" from ancient Greece to the early twentieth century, see Etienne Gilson, *The Unity of Philosophical Experience* (New York: Scribner, 1937).

15. On this subject, see Marcia L. Colish, *The Mirror of Language*, rev. ed. (Lincoln and London: University of Nebraska Press, 1983).

16. Lewis Carroll, *Through the Looking-Glass* (London: Macmillan, 1968), 130.

17. Paul Christianson, "Chaucer's Literacy," *Chaucer Review* 11 (1976–77): 122.

18. Alanus de Insulis, *De Incarnatione Dei (Rhythmus alter)*. Migne *Patrologia Latina*, no. 210, 579 (my translation).

19. "Framed stories" go back at least to 1600 B.C. For an interesting discussion of this genre and Chaucer's relation to it, see Robert A. Pratt and Karl Young, "The Literary Framework of the *Canterbury Tales*," in *Sources and Analogues of Chaucer's Canterbury Tales*, ed. W. F. Bryan and Germaine Dempster (1941; reprint, New York: Humanities Press, 1958), 1–81.

20. John Gardner, *The Poetry of Chaucer* (Carbondale: Southern Illinois University Press, 1977), chap. 7.

21. The question of art as knowledge has a long history. Hans Gadamer, in *Truth and Method* (New York: Crossroad Publishing, 1975), writes:

Thus imitation, as representation, has a clear cognitive function. Therefore the idea of imitation was able to continue in the theory of art for as long as the significance of art as knowledge was unquestioned. But that is valid only while it is held that knowledge of the true is knowledge of the essence, for art supports this kind of knowledge in a convincing way. For the nominalism of modern science, however, and its idea of reality, from which Kant drew the conclusion that aesthetics has nothing to do with knowledge, the concept of mimesis has lost its aesthetic force. (103–4)

22. For an informative discussion of the nature of medieval audience-author contract, see Robert B. Burlin, *Chaucerian Fiction* (Princeton, N.J.: Princeton University Press, 1977), 6–7.

23. See the seminal article of William Frost, "An Interpretation of Chau-

cer's *Knight's Tale*," *Review of English Studies* 25 (1949): 289–304; reprinted in *Chaucer Criticism, The Canterbury Tales: An Anthology,* ed. Richard J. Schoeck and Jerome Taylor (Notre Dame: University of Notre Dame Press, 1960).

24. For an interesting discussion of the relationship between iconography and Chaucer's poetry, see V. A. Kolve, *Chaucer and the Imagery of Narrative* (Stanford, Cal.: Stanford University Press, 1984).

25. See Robertson, *Preface to Chaucer*, 113.

26. This is the view of R. M. Lumiansky in *Of Sundry Folk: The Dramatic Principle in the Canterbury Tales* (Austin, Tex.: University of Texas Press, 1955), and others.

27. The lines read, "A husband should not be inquisitive of God's secrets, nor of his wife." Although *wyf* is not a genitive and, therefore, not possessive of *pryvetee*, the rhetorical force of the lines and the rest of the tale extend *pryvetee* to both wife and God.

28. *Paronomasia* (to name besides, call by a different name), from Greek *paranomazein, para* (beside, beyond) and *onuma* (name).

29. For a further discussion of the biblical and medical images of cleansing in the tale, see David Williams, "Radical Therapy in the *Miller's Tale*," *Chaucer Review* 15(1981): 227–35.

30. *The American Heritage Dictionary*, New College Edition (1978), s.v. *superstition*: "a belief that some action or circumstance not logically related to the course of events influences its outcome."

31. Burlin, *Chaucerian Fiction*, 219.

32. For a fuller discussion of authority and experience, see ibid., 3–22.

33. Ibid., 17.

34. Incubi were demons in male form thought to seek sexual congress with women during sleep: from Latin *incubare* (to lie upon). Succubi were demons in female form that sought sex with men while they slept: from Latin *succubare* (to lie underneath).

35. M. D. Chenu, *Toward Understanding St. Thomas*, trans. A. M. Landry and Dominic Hughes (Chicago: H. Regnery Co., 1964), 60–61.

36. For an excellent short article on this fascinating subject, see Douglas Wurtele, "Some Uses of Physiognomical Lore in Chaucer's *Canterbury Tales*," *Chaucer Review* 17(1982–83): 130–41.

37. *Encyclopaedia Universalis*, s.v. *Icone* (my translation).

38. Robert E. Nichols, Jr., "The Pardoner's Ale and Cake," *PMLA* 82(1967), 502.

39. See a summary of these interpretations and others in Robinson, *The Works of Geoffrey Chaucer*, 751–2.

40. See the interesting article of Douglas Wurtele, which presents a detailed argument concerning the relation of the *Parson's Tale* to the *Retraction,* "The Penitence of Geoffrey Chaucer," *Viator* 11(1980): 335—59.

41. See Corinne E. Kaufman, "Dame Pertelote's Parlous Parle," *Chaucer Review* 4 (1970): 41–48.

42. See, for example, Jill Mann, "The *Speculum Stultorum* and the *Nun's Priest's Tale,*" *Chaucer Review* 9 (1974–75): 262–82, and Susan Gallick, "Styles of Usage in the *Nun's Priest's Tale,*" *Chaucer Review* 11 (1976–77): 232–47.

43. Mortimer J. Donovan, "The *Moralite* of the Nun's Priest's Sermon," *Journal of English and German Philology* 52 (1953): 507.

44. Saul Nathaniel Brody, "Truth and Fiction in the *Nun's Priest's Tale,*" *Chaucer Review* 14 (1979–80): 33.

45. Walter J. Ong, "The Writer's Audience is Always a Fiction," *PMLA* 90(1975): 16.

Bibliography

Primary Sources

ROBINSON, F. N. *The Works of Geoffrey Chaucer.* 2d edition. Boston: Houghton Mifflin Co., 1962. Robinson's is the standard edition. It has a good glossary and helpful notes.

Secondary Sources

BURLIN, ROBERT B. *Chaucerian Fiction.* Princeton, N.J.: Princeton University Press, 1977. An indispensable study of the idea of fiction in Chaucer's work and its development through different phases of his work.

CESPEDES, FRANK V. "Chaucer's Pardoner and Preaching." *Journal of English Literary History* 44 (1977): 1–18. Shows how the Pardoner calls into question the validity of storytelling and sees the Pardoner and Parson as opposed extremes of fiction tellers.

COLISH, MARCIA L. *The Mirror of Language: A Study in the Medieval Theory of Knowledge.* Rev. ed. Lincoln and London: University of Nebraska Press, 1983. An excellent study of the complex question of the philosophy of language and the theories of cognition in the Middle Ages.

DAVID, ALFRED. *The Strumpet Muse: Art and Morals in Chaucer's Poetry.* Bloomington: Indiana University Press, 1976. Examines the tensions between principles of medieval philosophy and the production of good art, concluding that they were not resolved by Chaucer.

DONALDSON, E. TALBOT. "Chaucer's Three P's: Pandarus, Pardoner, and Poet." *Michigan Quarterly Review* 14 (1975): 282–301. A discussion of the Pardoner and Pandarus as manifestations of the poet.

FRIEDMAN, JOHN BLOCK. "The *Nun's Priest's Tale*: The Preacher and the Mermaid's Song." *Chaucer Review* 7 (1972–73): 250–266. An interesting discussion of the iconographic dimension in Chaucer's poetry.

GALLICK, SUSAN. "Styles of Usage in the *Nun's Priest's Tale.*" *Chaucer Review* 11 (1976–77): 232–47. The *Nun's Priest's Tale* is essentially parody—the parody of rhetoric and language.

GARDNER, JOHN CHAMPLIN. *The Poetry of Chaucer.* Carbondale: Southern Illinois University Press, 1977. A comprehensive and sensitive study of Chaucer's poetry and the cultural influences on it.

HARWOOD, BRITTON J. "Language and the Real: Chaucer's Manciple." *Chaucer Review* 6 (1971–72): 268–79. Discusses the relation of personal order / disorder to the order / disorder reflected in the tales.

HOWARD, DONALD R. *The Idea of the Canterbury Tales.* Berkeley: University of California Press, 1976. The thesis is that the *Canterbury Tales* should be read as intentionally unfinished and thus complete.

HOFFMAN, ARTHUR W. "Chaucer's Prologue to Pilgrimage: The Two Voices." *Journal of English Literary History* 21 (1954): 1–16. Reprinted in *Chaucer: Modern Essays in Criticism.* Edited by Edward C. Wagenknecht. New York: Oxford University Press, 1959. An informative and sensitive study of the poetic unity of the portraits of the pilgrims in the *General Prologue,* and its unity to the whole of the *Canterbury Tales.*

JORDAN, ROBERT M. *Chaucer and the Shape of Creation: The Aesthetic Possibilities of Inorganic Structure.* Cambridge, Mass.: Harvard University Press, 1967. An important study of Chaucer's worldview and its reflection in his poetry.

KHINOY, STEPHEN A. "Inside Chaucer's Pardoner." *Chaucer Review* 6 (1971–72): 255–67. One of the richest discussions of the figure of the Pardoner exploring Chaucer's use of the theory of language and fiction and their relation to reality.

KISER, LISA J. *Telling Classical Tales: Chaucer and the "Legend of Good Women."* Ithaca, N.Y.: Cornell University Press, 1983. Although not a study of the *Canterbury Tales,* a persuasive and intelligent discussion of Chaucer's motives and methods in poetry.

LAWLOR, JOHN. *Chaucer.* London: Hutchinson; New York: Harper, 1968. A discussion of Chaucer's works from the point of view of his narrative art and the oral nature of his poetry.

LEITCH, L. M. "Sentence and Solaas: The Function of the Host in the *Canterbury Tales.*" *Chaucer Review* 17 (1982–83): 5–20. A discussion of the function of game and mirth in relation to serious content, and Harry Bailly's preference for entertainment.

LORD, URSULA. "Literary Self-Reflexivity in the *Canterbury Tales.*" Master's thesis, McGill University, 1984. In a study of several of the tales, Lord illustrates Chaucer's claim for the autonomy of literary art from didacticism.

MANN, JILL. "The *Speculum Stultorum* and the *Nun's Priest's Tale.*" *Chaucer Review* 9 (1974–75), 262–82. True morality, intellectualism, and eloquence are seen as inaccessible in the *Nun's Priest's Tale.*

McALPINE, MONICA E. "The Pardoner's Homosexuality and How it Matters." *PMLA* 95 (1980): 8–22. A very useful discussion of Chaucer's portrayal of the Pardoner as a homosexual and the extension of the idea of sexual contradiction to spiritual contradiction. As the Pardoner's body contradicts itself, so his relics annihilate their own efficacy through his use of them.

MILLER, ROBERT P. "Allegory in the *Canterbury Tales*." *Companion to Chaucer Studies*. Edited by Beryl Rowland. Toronto: Oxford University Press, 1968, 268–90. An informative discussion of Chaucer's use of allegory in the *Canterbury Tales*.

———. "Chaucer's Pardoner: The Scriptural Eunuch and the *Pardoner's Tale*." *Speculum* 30 (1955): 180–99. Reprinted in *Chaucer Criticism, Vol. 1: The Canterbury Tales: An Anthology*. Edited by Richard J. Schoeck and Jerome Taylor. Notre Dame: University of Notre Dame Press, 1960. A seminal study of Chaucer's use of Scriptural reference in creating the Pardoner. An indispensable article for any study of the Pardoner or Chaucer's use of scripture.

NICHOLS, ROBERT E. "The Pardoner's Ale and Cake." *PMLA* 82 (1967): 498–504. An informative discussion of the use of food and the Eucharist symbolism in the *Pardoner's Tale*.

OWEN, W. J. B. "The Old Man in the *Pardoner's Tale*." *Review of English Studies* 2 (1951): 49–55. Reprinted in *Chaucer: Modern Essays in Criticism*. Edited by Edward C. Wagenknecht. New York: Oxford University Press, 1959. An informative discussion of the interpretation of the old man as Death, and the sources from which Chaucer drew his portrayal of the figure.

PATTERSON, LEE W. "Chaucerian Confession: Penitential Literature and the Pardoner." *Medievalia et Humanistica* 7 (1976): 153–73. Discusses the Pardoner as one who creates a fictive self to hide an unbearable real self.

REISS, EDMUND. "The Final Irony of the *Pardoner's Tale*." *College English* 25 (1964): 260–66. Unlike Chaucer's use of irony through characters revealing more than they intend, in the *Pardoner's Prologue* irony arises out of the character's revealing less than he intends because of the nature of language and audience.

ROBERTSON, D. W., JR. *A Preface to Chaucer: Studies in Medieval Perspective*. Princeton: Princeton University Press, 1963. An indispensable study of Chaucer's intellectual and cultural milieu and its influence on his poetry.

ROWLAND, BERYL. "Chaucer's Idea of the Pardoner." *Chaucer Review* 14 (1979–80): 140–154. An interesting analysis of the sexual metaphor in the portrayal of the Pardoner, wherein he is seen as hermaphrodite, rather than merely homosexual, in order that many other dualities in the Pardoner's prologue and tale can be conveyed through the metaphor of fundamental duality.

RUGGIERS, PAUL G. *The Art of the Canterbury Tales.* Madison: University of Wisconsin Press, 1965. A very informative study of the artistic achievement of the *Canterbury Tales.*

STEVENS, MARTIN AND KATHLEEN FALVEY. "Substance, Accident, and Transformation: A Reading of the *Pardoner's Tale.*" *Chaucer Review* 17 (1982–83): 142–58. Discusses the imagery of transformation, including the transformation of language and the Eucharist, and sees the Pardoner's world as one of excrement.

WASSERMAN, JULIAN N. "The Ideal and the Actual: The Philosophical Unity of *Canterbury Tales,* Ms. Group III." *Allegorica* 7, no. 2 (1982): 65–99. One of the best recent studies on realism and nominalism in the *Canterbury Tales,* particularly as they relate to Group III. Notes and bibliography in this article are essential reference for this subject.

WOOD, CHAUNCEY. *Chaucer and the Country of the Stars: Poetic Uses of Astrological Imagery.* Princeton: Princeton University Press, 1970. A study of the medieval science of astrology and how it informs the thought and imagery of Chaucer's work.

WURTELE, DOUGLAS. "The Penitence of Geoffrey Chaucer." *Viator* 11 (1980): 335–59. An intelligent and provocative study linking the *Retraction* to the *Parson's Tale* and vice versa, and revealing the literary dimensions of the theme of penitence in the *Canterbury Tales.*

Index

About the Author

David Williams is chairman of the English department at McGill University, where he teaches Chaucer and Anglo-Saxon. He has published *Cain and Beowulf: A Study in Secular Allegory* (Toronto: University of Toronto Press, 1982) and articles on Chaucer and the literature of the Middle Ages. His interests lie in the medieval concept of the monstrous and the grotesque and its expression in literature and art. Professor Williams attended the Pontifical Institute of Mediaeval Studies in Toronto and received his Ph.D. in English from the University of Toronto.